Prisca Middlemiss is a freelance writer specializing in family and child health. She has been a regular contributor to *Practical Parenting* since its first issue and has researched and written its monthly Medifile column since 1988. She also researches and writes its monthly health news page. She has written widely on children's behaviour, family matters and early years education and has contributed regularly to a wide range of parenting and specialist early years titles. She started in journalism as editor of the British Diabetic Association journal *Balance*. She then joined the staff of the doctors' newspaper *Medical News* and then *General Practitioner* where she became science commissioning editor. She lives in west London with her husband and two children, both of whom were catastrophically awful sleepers.

PRACTICAL
parenting

Baby & toddler sleep action plans

Prisca Middlemiss

PAN BOOKS

First published as *Sleep* 1999 by Pan Books

This edition published 2001 by Pan Books
an imprint of Macmillan Publishers Ltd
25 Eccleston Place, London SW1W 9NF
Basingstoke and Oxford
Associated companies throughout the world
www.macmillan.com

ISBN 0 330 39993 4

Copyright © Prisca Middlemiss 1999

The right of Prisca Middlemiss to be identified as the author of this work has been asserted by her in accordance with the Copyright, Designs and Patents Act 1988.

All rights reserved. No part of this publication may be reproduced, stored in or introduced into a retrieval system, or transmitted, in any form, or by any means (electronic, mechanical, photocopying, recording or otherwise) without the prior written permission of the publisher. Any person who does any unauthorized act in relation to this publication may be liable to criminal prosecution and civil claims for damages.

1 3 5 7 9 8 6 4 2

A CIP catalogue record for this book is available from the British Library.

Typeset by SetSystems Ltd, Saffron Walden, Essex
Printed and bound in Great Britain by
Mackays of Chatham plc, Chatham, Kent

This book is sold subject to the condition that it shall not, by way of trade or otherwise, be lent, re-sold, hired out, or otherwise circulated without the publisher's prior consent in any form of binding or cover other than that in which it is published and without a similar condition including this condition being imposed on the subsequent purchaser.

Practical Parenting is published monthly by IPC Media Ltd, King's Reach Tower, Stamford Street, London SE1 9LS. For subscription enquiries and overseas orders call 01444 445555. Alternatively, you can call the subscriptions credit card hotline (UK orders only) on 01622 778778.

Contents

Acknowledgements

The author would like to thank all the individuals and organizations who helped in putting this guide together, in particular: Tracey Atkins; Deborah Jackson; Dr David Bramble; Dr Bryan Lask; Dr Gregory Stores; Glenys Sykes; Professor Dieter Wolke; Jeanine Young; Enuresis Research and Information Centre; Foundation for the Study of Infant Deaths; MENSA; National Asthma Campaign; Sleep Scotland; The Steele Road Mother-and-Toddler Club

Introduction

> Maria, mother of Martha, three and a half, and Jacob, eighteen months: *'I had such a feeling of dread as the night approached. I totally lost confidence in my ability to cope. My God, I used to think, the night's coming. It was a huge problem. We tried everything, early nights, late nights, bringing her in with us in the morning, giving her a bottle of milk – but nothing worked. In the end we did sleep training – and it worked in four nights!'*

An undisturbed night's sleep – remember it? Or does the memory belong, with evenings out and carefree clothes shopping, to the days before you became a parent? Is bedtime in your home an orderly routine, followed by lights out and silence – or is it an extended battle zone? And wonderful as it is to welcome warm little bodies under the duvet in the small hours, do you ever hanker for extra space to snooze, or for the days when *you* chose who you slept with?

Then join the other millions. The Royal College of Psychiatrists has said there is evidence that one-quarter of all children aged between one and three have severe sleeping problems. According to the Children of the Nineties study two-thirds of parents of eighteen-month-old toddlers were woken regularly in the past year. Almost one family in five was woken more than once a night; one family in fourteen was woken three or more times. At the very least, two million parents of children under five are woken in the night by their sleepless children.

Don't despair. Most parents find a gradual improvement during the pre-school years, especially in waking at night. But there's no doubt that sleep difficulties *can* last for months and even years.

'However bad it is, remember that it won't last.'

On the face of it, it's crazy. Adults need less than half the amount of sleep that a newborn baby needs. They need two-thirds the amount a five-year-old needs. Recent findings from the Sleep Research Laboratory at Loughborough University, under Britain's top sleep researcher, Professor Jim Horne, show that on average women slept seven and a half hours a day, men seven and a quarter. An average baby, by contrast, sleeps around fourteen hours a day.

But who says your baby is average? Research in the USA has shown this gradient:

Age	*Average sleep needs*
Newborn	16–17 hours
Four months	14–15 hours
Six–eight months	13–14 hours
Twelve months	13½ hours
Two years	13 hours
Three years	12 hours
Five years	11 hours

Just imagine sitting there timing your baby's sleep! Some people can think of better things to do. Anyway, the question isn't really how much sleep a baby or child needs, it's when. Why is it that the people shopping in the early hours at all-night supermarkets are not insomniacs and all-night ravers but parents with their sleepless babies?

It's for two reasons. First, babies don't get the message about days and nights until they are three to four months old. Second, sleep goes in cycles between deep and shallow levels and babies' cycles are different from adults. Adults spend 75–80 per cent of their sleeping time in deep sleep and only 20–25 per cent of their sleep time in shallow dreaming or so-called REM (Rapid Eye Movement) sleep: if you lift the lids you can see the eyes darting and jerking around.

Adults have about five sleep cycles a night, dropping into deep sleep and then surfacing into shallow REM sleep approximately every ninety minutes. Babies' sleep cycles are different:

- At birth, each cycle only lasts around fifty minutes.
- Babies spend far more time in shallow REM sleep. The precise reason isn't known, but it's thought that REM sleep stimulates the maturing brain to develop. In the womb your baby may have as many as fifteen hours of REM sleep a day. A two-months premature baby sleeps most of the day, spending 80 per cent of his sleep time in REM sleep. REM sleep drops to 67 per cent by one month pre-term and full-term newborn babies split their sleep evenly – half in REM sleep and half in deeper sleep. The amount of shallower REM sleep continues to fall – to four hours by your baby's first birthday and to three hours by the age of three.
- Newborns drift first into shallow REM sleep and stay there for

up to an hour before descending into deeper sleep. Adults drop more quickly into deep sleep. Over the first three months, the baby pattern becomes more like an adult pattern.

- Early in the night there's more deep sleep and less REM sleep, in babies as in adults. But babies may also have a late burst of deep sleep at the end of an all-night stint.

So what? Well, so a lot – because babies wake much more easily from REM sleep than from deep sleep. But once babies mature to an adult shallow/deep sleep pattern, why don't they stay asleep like adults? Infra-red all-night video has revealed the truth: all babies, good sleepers and bad, wake at night during shallow sleep. But while good sleepers drift off again, hugging a toy, sucking their thumbs or just looking around, poor sleepers can't settle. Instead they cry, call for attention or arrive expectantly at their parents' bedside.

So that's it. All you have to do is teach your child to settle himself back to sleep. But there is more to it than that. As any parent of more than one child will tell you, your baby's temperament is a key player in how well or badly he sleeps. Research by psychologists at Reading University has shown clearly that children with sleep problems are likely to have a more 'difficult' temperament and to be less adaptable.

Your personal circumstances have a bearing as well. Anyone can let a baby grizzle himself to sleep in the seclusion of a well-built semi. But what if your walls are paper-thin? And if you've been out at work all day or you're coping as a lone parent, nightly fights at bedtime may not seem a good idea.

You need your sleep. In the exciting days of new parenthood, a few disrupted nights can shift you into overdrive – that paradoxical feeling where your eyes sting with tiredness, but you're raring for more. Long-term sleep fragmentation – where the refreshing 'core' sleep you really need is interrupted night after night – can be serious, plunging you into anxiety, apathy and even violence – all the feelings you'd normally associate with depression. You may well be depressed, but you're chronically short of sleep as well. Sex, your social life, enjoying your children – all these go headlong. Marriages suffer.

Your child, too, needs sleep so she isn't miserable next day. Children who are short of sleep aren't very different from adults: they can't concentrate, they're irritable, short-tempered and aggressive.

I have drawn on parents' experiences of disrupted nights, picked my way through the sleep research and asked experts for ideas. This problem-solving guide is the result. I hope it shows you the very simple and effective methods you can use to get your child to go to bed, stay in bed, sleep and be happy.

Key Points

- Every night young children wake more than two million people from sleep.
- People who don't get enough deep sleep get the same feelings as if they were depressed.
- New babies have more shallow sleep than adults.
- When babies are sleeping lightly they wake easily.
- Babies and young children can learn to fall asleep without bothering you.

1

The first six months: what to expect

The best approach to sleep and wakefulness in your baby's first weeks is to expect the worst! You're bound to have disturbed nights. But you might have a pleasant surprise when your baby drifts off after a feed, cries to be fed at two- to four-hour intervals and stays asleep for more than twenty minutes at a stretch.

In the early weeks your baby needs to know that you are there when she cries for food, comfort, security and warmth. This means round-the-clock duties, so you too need a rest. These ways work for some people:

- Take your baby into bed with you and sleep together (*but* see Bedsharing, page 11).
- Express your milk and share the night feeds with your partner. You do the 11pm to 3am shift and he does 3am to 7am. It means your baby has to use a bottle, but it's still breast milk.
- If your partner's at work and you're on maternity leave, he does the evening care while you get some sleep ready for the night. This is good if you have a colicky baby (see 'Colic', page 10).
- Powernap. Mid-afternoon, between 2pm and 5pm, is when

your body cycle takes a natural dip, making microsleeps easier. Professor Jim Horne, Britain's leading sleep researcher and author of *Why We Sleep*, said recently that the natural sleep pattern for adults is a long stretch at night and an afternoon siesta-style shut-eye.

- If you're not the powernapping type, relax, feet up.
- If you've a generous relative who wants to buy you a present, or you've got the spare cash, buy in help. Local family activity or National Childbirth Trust magazines are good sources of contacts. Your baby clinic or doctor's surgery may have a noticeboard where you can advertise. Or ask your Health Visitor.
- *Remember*: your body most needs its core sleep – the first four to five hours of the night. So long as you get this, in a usually unbroken stretch, you can keep going.

Meanwhile, what is your baby up to?

New babies

New babies sleep for twelve to twenty hours a day, and often less than you were hoping for. Mostly at first it's just feed, sleep and wake and sometimes if you are breastfeeding it seems to be non-stop feeding.

> Glenys Sykes, a Health Visitor, says: *'For the first three or four weeks there is no routine and don't be full of anxiety about setting one. Watch your baby for signs of an emerging routine and let him set the pace.'*

- Let your baby listen to soothing sounds as she falls asleep. White noise (radio off station), womb-music tapes, musical mobiles, or quiet classical music work well. Try your favourite music. Remember – she's been listening for the last three months of pregnancy, even through a sea of amniotic fluid. Your voice too will soothe her as she already knows it well.

By two months

Your baby spends less time in shallow sleep with more deep sleep. She may wake now before she is really hungry and look around or play. Daytime sleeps (usually two to four) are developing – anything from infuriatingly short catnaps to long sleeps that let you catch up. Your baby may sleep more at night, even a full four to six hours. Your baby can soothe herself to sleep (in fact, from three weeks).

- Note when your baby drifts off in the evening. Whenever it is, pick this as the official bedtime.

By three to four months

Your baby's sleep–wake cycle should be roughly synchronized to yours by now. If you're in real luck, your baby will even manage five or six hours' sleep at night or just wake once. Your baby may start phases of being wakeful at night. It could be a growth spurt, or you may never know why.

> Chris, mother of two-year-old Oscar, says: *'As a baby Oscar woke up every four hours on the dot. Then at three months for about a month or six weeks he would stay awake and wouldn't go back to sleep unless I walked him round and round the room. My arms grew visibly longer!'*

- You can start to get real routine back into your life now.

By five to six months

A clear day–night pattern may have emerged, with your baby taking a longer sleep at night and two daytime naps, each lasting one to two hours. However, your baby is still surfacing at night – anything up to eight times. Some babies go through a tricky phase with a third daytime nap which they don't really need but can't quite get through the day without, leading to very late bedtimes.

- You can now teach your baby to sleep through the night.

  According to Dr David Bramble, Queen's Medical Centre, Nottingham, *'More than 95 per cent of children, including severely learning disabled children, are physiologically capable of sleeping through the night at six months of age.'*

Colic

Colicky babies fret more than others and have an agonized, high-pitched cry and more screaming bouts. They often cry longest and most inconsolably in the evening, sometimes after or during their feed. You soothe them the way that works best – feeding (even if it's only half an hour since the last feed), offering boiled and cooled water, giving extra sucking time, laying tummy down and rubbing or patting the baby's back, undressing for a massage, burping, trying a warm bath, the colic dance (swaying rhythmically from one foot to the other while holding your baby), a ride in the car, or peace and quiet in the cot after all this stimulation. Colicky babies may never learn to settle themselves to sleep. You may find the prospect of yet more screaming too horrendous to allow them even to try.

If you can't find a reason for the crying, do ask your doctor to check your baby over.

- Contact Serene [formerly CRY-SIS] (see 'Who can help' page 108).
- Paediatric osteopathy (one to four sessions are usually enough) is said to help colic by easing structures at the base of the skull and possibly releasing pressures on nerves and blood vessels.
- Be patient: the screaming will ease – often around three to four months. Then let your baby learn to settle alone.

Should I let her sleep in my bed?

It's a good idea to keep your baby in her cot beside your bed for the first six months. If you have her in your bed:

- You can comfort your baby easily.
- You are more likely to wake when your baby does or when she's sleeping lightly.
- You are more likely to breastfeed your baby more often. Evidence from the Sebastian Diamond Mother and Baby Sleep Laboratory in Bristol shows that when mothers shared beds with their babies, they breastfed them twice as often (four times a night) but the total feeding time was only a little longer. The night suckling is good for breastfeeding as it

stimulates your breastfeeding hormone prolactin and brings on your milk supply.
- You will be responsive to your baby's condition and can feel her to reassure yourself that she is the right temperature and her breathing movements are regular.

But:

- Your alertness to your baby may stop you from sleeping restfully.
- As your baby grows she will become more active and wriggly and disturb your sleep more.
- Falling asleep with you prevents your baby from learning how to fall asleep alone.
- Your baby could get hot. Recent research from Bristol shows that babies' skin temperature might be higher if they shared beds, but their core temperature was not even when babies slept on top of their mothers or in direct contact with them. But it is important not to cover babies' heads or to let bedding cover their heads.
- It isn't possible to have your baby in bed with you *and* follow advice on reducing the risk of cot death. The Foundation for the Study of Infant Deaths (FSID) suggests that you breastfeed and play with your baby in bed but put her in her own cot to sleep.

Some people feel very strongly about bedsharing. Deborah Jackson wrote *Three in a Bed* because people made her feel guilty about it.

She says: *'Here in the West we often think we have a problem when a baby or young child craves our company at night. In almost every culture throughout mankind's history parents have slept with their children as the solution to meeting their night-time needs. I believe it helps us all pay attention to the root causes of why our children cry.'*

Mary Daly, professional officer with the Community Practitioners and Health Visitors Association, is supportive.

'Children may need to be comforted in bed by their parents and for babies sharing a bed is extremely helpful for establishing and maintaining breastfeeding. For a longer sleep your child could be returned to its own cot or bed. The issue is not about bedsharing or not. What is most important is that a distressed infant has his needs for close physical comfort met.'

There are times when you shouldn't sleep with your baby:

- If you or your partner smoke.
- If you've had an alcoholic drink.
- If you've taken sleeping tablets or anything that might make you sleep more deeply than normal.
- If you are unwell. Not only are you more likely to infect your baby, but you are less likely to react to her.
- On a put-you-up or sofa.

If your baby does bedshare, a time will come eventually when you want her to stay in her own bed.

- Make the change gradual.
- Lay a piece of your clothing in her bed and make sure she has her comforter.
- Suggest that she's not quite old enough to have her own cot/bed. She may want to prove herself to you.

- If she returns to your bed in the middle of the night, take her firmly back.
- Stay determined once you have made the change. If she's unwell, stay with her but make it plain that from now on your bed isn't hers.
- Allow her in with you in the morning.

And don't leave the change too late.

Eddie is the middle of three boys. He's four and a half and still spends every night in his parents' bed. At nine months he wouldn't settle in his cot and his mother Jane took him into her bed. At first it was nice; Eddie loved the contact and slept well. Four years on Jane has had enough:

> 'I should try to get him into his own bed but the thought of all the struggle and crying is too much. I'd rather get what little sleep I can. Last night was the last straw. He wet our bed. It was the ultimate insult. At 4am we all got up and changed the sheets and tried to settle back to sleep. But Eddie woke and started muttering, so I never slept at all. When he puts his arms and legs round me in a lock, I ask him, "Why don't you sleep in your bed?" And he answers, "There's not enough people in it."'

Cot death

In your baby's early months it's natural to worry about cot death. It's because of people being aware and putting babies down to sleep on their backs that cot death is now so uncommon. The number of babies dying suddenly and unexpectedly in their sleep in the past ten years in the UK has fallen sharply – from over 1500 a year to under 500.

Researchers, the FSID and the UK Department of Health all believe that this is a direct result of their advice. Joyce Epstein, from the FSID, says:

> *'There has never been a safer time to have a baby. But ten babies are still dying every week silently and unexpectedly and until we know what causes cot death, all parents and carers should follow the reduce the risk advice. While it comes with no guarantee, we know that it has more than halved the rate of cot death. But don't let the fear of cot death stop you enjoying your baby.'*

This is the official advice on risk reduction:

- **Place your baby on the back to sleep**
  Why? The exact reason isn't known, but cot death is much less common among babies who sleep on their backs.
  Won't she choke? A normal, healthy baby won't choke.
  Won't she roll over? By the time she's able to roll over at five or six months she's already at less risk of cot death. If you find your baby on her tummy, gently turn her over but don't feel you should check constantly.
- **Cut smoking in pregnancy – fathers too**
  Babies do best in a smoke-free zone – from the moment of conception on. In a recent study doctors have confirmed that two-thirds of babies who die from cot death could have been saved if their parents didn't smoke. Even someone who finished a cigarette within the past hour shouldn't be close to your baby.
- **Don't let your baby get too hot**
  What's too hot? You can tell if your baby's too hot by feeling

her tummy. She'll be sweating or look flushed. It's especially important not to let your baby get too hot when she has an infection.

How can I be sure she doesn't get too hot at night? Keep the temperature in the bedroom even, at a comfortable temperature of about 18°C (65°F).

Does that mean she can't be 'nested' in something warm? It does. There shouldn't be anything in the cot with her that could make her overheat – like a baby nest, a cot bumper or duvet or a sheepskin or hot-water bottle. If she's to sleep in a sleeping bag, it should be maximum 1 tog rating and be sleeveless. And you shouldn't swaddle her.

- **Keep your baby's head uncovered – place your baby in the 'feet to foot' position**
  A study has shown that one cot death baby in five was found with her head covered by bedclothes. Keeping the head uncovered also allows your baby to lose excess heat.
- **If your baby is unwell, seek medical advice promptly.**

But not all babies will sleep on their backs

Louise, mother of Olivia, six months, says: *'Olivia simply wouldn't sleep on her back. I tried everything but after thirty minutes her legs would be flicking about kicking her bedclothes. As soon as I put her on her tummy she settled happily. Her Health Visitor said I shouldn't let her sleep on her tummy. But Olivia was much happier and from the early days she could move her head from side to side if she needed to. So I got fanatical about other things. Olivia has a new mattress, I make sure her feet are at the bottom of the cot and the blankets only reach to her waist, though now she's six months old she pushes her way up the cot. I'm very firm about her not being overheated, and no one smokes anywhere near her.'*

- The FSID stresses that you shouldn't pick and choose which bits of cot death advice you follow to reduce the risk – you should follow them all.

When can I stop worrying about cot death?

Don't worry about it! If you do, you risk becoming over-anxious and tending to your baby's every whimper when she stirs, just causing problems later when your baby learns to expect attention for a slight whimper or grizzle. Having said that, cot death is bound to remain a background concern. Four times out of five it occurs before your baby is six months old with the peak age between two and four months. Beyond nine months it is very rare.

Premature babies

Some parents complain that premature babies are restless sleepers after the first few weeks when they are so drowsy you have to wake them to feed. But researchers found just the opposite – that pre-term babies' day–night cycles matured earlier than in full-term babies and that good sleep habits learned on the neonatal unit set the premature babies up for life at home.

> Kirsten, twenty-two months, is one such baby. Her mother Ann says: *'Kirsten was born at thirty weeks (I had pre-eclampsia) so she spent eight weeks in SCBU and it gave her very good training because she was used to sleeping on her own from the start. Even now she hates coming into our bed – wonderful!'*

If you have a restless baby who was premature, it may be because:

- She's a normally wakeful baby – just different from the sleepy baby of the first weeks.
- Very premature babies do cry more during the day at three to six months.
- You go on waking her at night for longer than she needs and being woken may interfere with her developing night–day cycle – she may miss the frequent handling.
- Once the early, vulnerable months are over, your natural concern gets in the way of her need for a loving but firm approach. This is especially true if your baby had times in hospital when she stopped breathing and came home with an apnoea (breathing) monitor.

A recent study of babies in Finland and Germany by Professor Dieter Wolke at the University of Hertfordshire showed that premature babies sleep through the night earlier than full-term babies. Why? Because they are more likely to be bottle-fed. Of course breast milk is even more important for premature babies than for full-term babies in preventing infections and helping long-term development. But this research shows that there are things you can do to help your premature baby sleep better. Here are some:

- In hospital, hold your baby skin-to-skin against your chest. This is called kangaroo care and helps in lots of ways – improving your milk flow, calming crying, improving your baby's breathing and increasing the time she spends deeply asleep.
- Keep to the good sleep habits your baby learned in hospital.
- If your baby finds silence unsettling, play gentle classical music. One family audiotaped sounds on the neonatal unit and played the tape to their baby at home.
- Stay in contact with a support group to share experiences. Many neonatal units have a support group, or contact BLISS (see 'Who can help', page 108).

Every family finds its own way through this difficult period. For some, the joy that their baby is well matters more than losing sleep, as the following story shows.

Kieran, three and a quarter, has only slept through the night once in his life. He normally sleeps in his parents' bed. His mother, Paulette ('sleep deprivation is my middle name'), is happy but tired. *'Having the children may mean sacrifices. I lost my daughter at twenty-six weeks and then Kieran was born at twenty-six weeks. He was very lively and even though they dimmed the lights at night on the neonatal intensive care unit, with all the noise and activity he never settled into a sleep routine. He came home when he was two months old being demand-fed every hour and a half. So of course he had to sleep in our bed. Yes, we have spoilt him rotten but bonding is very, very important. Kieran came home with an apnoea monitor, but one night the batteries ran low so I took it off for good. I was naturally worried about cot death so I was tuned in to his breathing and his sleeping patterns. When he was about eighteen months I tried to leave him to cry but he made himself sick and I couldn't stand it. He was too precious. His consultant warned us that as he was premature he might well have sleeping problems and when I asked for how long he said, "Oh, until he's three or four." He was right!'*

Key points

- To be a good parent you need four or five hours of unbroken sleep most nights.
- In the early weeks your baby needs to learn the confidence that you will meet her needs for food, love and warmth.
- By two months at the latest your baby can soothe herself to sleep. Let her try!
- You can start a regular bedtime routine from two months.
- In the first six months babies progress from non-stop wake–feed–sleep cycles to being perfectly able to sleep through the night.
- If your baby shares your bed, you may sleep more lightly.
- You can't have your baby in your bed and follow all the advice on reducing the risk of cot death. Put your baby back in her cot by your bed after feeding, the Foundation for the Study of Infant Deaths advises.
- Premature babies learn good sleep habits in hospital.

2
Settling into a routine

As your baby's sleeping patterns fall into a routine, you can help her to learn good habits. Then she won't fall asleep in ways that seem easy at the time but are difficult to change later.

What can you do in the early weeks?

Ann, mother of Fraser, five weeks, says: *Fraser wakes about twice a night. I don't speak to him, I just feed and change him and give him no attention so he gets the message. It's always dark so there isn't a lot to stay awake for.'*

- Let your baby know when it's night and day. Even in the womb, she knew about night–day differences. Keep night lighting low or off.
- Have a different sleeping place for daytime and night-time. For daytime sleeps keep the curtains open and let your baby sleep in different places – her car seat, a Moses basket or a carrycot downstairs, or a sling.
- Keep night-time surroundings in her cot – bedding, mobile, toys – reassuringly familiar.
- Never let your baby fall asleep on breast or bottle. It's a hard habit to break.

- Make the night feeds easy on yourself. Have your baby close to your bed so you can pick her up easily (see page 25). If she's bottle-fed, have the bottle ready made up in the fridge and a flask of hot water ready to warm it up. Only change her nappy if you have to – if she develops nappy rash. Make her day feeds quite different. Feed and change her downstairs, with family activities going on all round.

  Tip: To be sure to stay awake until the end of the feed, play story tapes to yourself on a Walkman while feeding.

Why does routine matter?

Routines help babies to sleep. In the days before electric lighting, our bodies took their cues about sleeping from the sunlight. Eskimos had a natural six-hour sleep in the summer and fourteen in the winter. We can still sense our own dependence on daylight when we wake earlier in spring but can't drag ourselves out of bed in winter. Light-dependence helps to explain why the all-day rhythms of people kept away from natural light–dark changes free-run to twenty-four and a half or twenty-five hours.

Daylight is just one of the clues we need to keep to our twenty-four hour cycle. The other clues are a routine – predictable mealtimes, getting-up times and bedtimes.

When does a routine start?

This is very variable. Some babies pick up routines from the early days, others are six months old. When you think about a routine, most people start at the beginning of the day. For babies, it's usually better to start with bedtime. As Health Visitor Glenys Sykes says:

> *'The bedtime routine is the lynchpin. Your baby discovers that his bed is a safe place to shut his eyes and fall asleep in.'*

Good bedtimes matter

- Through secure bedtimes a baby or child learns that it is safe to fall asleep.
- Through regular bedtimes the body clock is reset for the next twenty-four hours.

The time you choose for bedtime doesn't matter so much, as long as it's approximately the same every night and your baby isn't overtired when you start.

> Chris says: *'It was important to have a strong evening routine from six months. It could be at 5pm or at 7pm, but the routine was always the same. It takes an hour, we finish tea, put the toys away, run the bath, have the bath, have a bottle of milk, a story on the end of his bed, then lights out.'*

Suggested bedtime for a baby

- Make an event of it. First clear distractions. Put a *Don't disturb* notice on the front door and unplug the telephone.
- Prepare what you need – bathing things if she's going to have a bath, nightclothes, her nappy, a bottle.
- Give her a warm bath (if she likes it) and let her splash and play.
- Pat her dry on a pre-warmed towel. Then massage her with light baby oil. Add a drop of lavender oil to calm her.
- Put on a clean nappy and nightclothes.
- Give her final feed in the room where she'll sleep. Keep the lights dimmed and the curtains closed. Let her feed slowly if she wants but if she starts to play, bring it to a close.
- Put her in her cot. Sing her a lullaby if you like. Check the room is the same as it will be if she wakes in the night. Check the baby monitor is on.
- Say something calm and reassuring like 'Night night. Mummy's close.' Then leave.

Can I stop her waking in the night?

Not yet, because until she is around six months old she can't sleep through the night without more milk. But you can teach her that at night you'll meet her needs, but no more. When you're sure she's fed, warm and clean, give her a chance to settle on her own. If she's still crying after two or three minutes or you can hear that she's winding herself up, pick her up and settle her on your shoulder or in your arms, but stay by her cot. Once she's quiet, put her back in her cot and if she starts to cry again, don't pick her up for two or three more minutes. Stay where she can see you (perhaps in bed next to her), pat or rub her back and if it's dark, talk or sing softly. If she's getting increasingly frantic and you have to pick her up again, calm her as quickly as you can and put her back.

I know I shouldn't always nurse or rock her to sleep. So how should she get to sleep?

Lay her gently in her cot while she's drowsy but not asleep. This way she'll drop off on her own, a skill that she'll need when she wakes again. Of course you won't always do this, especially if your baby is a very sucky one; what matters is that she sometimes drops off without a nipple or teat in her mouth. Some babies with easy natures don't mind if they fall asleep on the breast or alone but most mind a lot. As for rocking and patting, rhythmic movement *does* help little babies to fall asleep but don't rock her every time or she'll always expect it. Choose a day when she's obviously tired to break the link in her mind.

> *'The best piece of advice to give new mothers is to leave the baby in the cot to settle themselves alone. They grizzle for ten to fifteen minutes. That's all.'*

Can I help her to fall asleep at all?

Offer her a cuddly. Your baby's hand may already be squeezing her blanket or stroking its silky edge. Place a thumb or finger in sucking position or, if you prefer, a dummy. These are 'transitional objects', standing in for you when you can't be there.

If she's wakeful, could it be cows' milk allergy?

If you think that your baby is sleeping restlessly because he's reacting to his milk or to allergens in your breast milk, consult your doctor. Restless sleep is unlikely to be your baby's only allergy symptom – she might well have eczema too. If you drink more than six cups a day of drinks like tea, cocoa, coffee and cola, the caffeine will mount up in your baby and make her wakeful. Once you stop caffeine drinks, she'll be herself again in a few days. Alcohol makes some babies irritable.

When can she safely sleep through?

'Through the night' really means a stretch of about six to eight hours, which may start at your bedtime and continue until you get up, or begin in the early evening and end, uncomfortably, at one or two o'clock in the morning. For many families there is a longish, just bearable phase when 'through the night' means from around eight or nine at night to four or five in the morning. There is a direct trade-off then between free evenings and a lie-in!

Once your baby is six months old – sometimes sooner, sometimes later – she can cope without a night feed. Watch for signs that she is ready, like these two families.

Alison, mother of Freddie, then five and a half months, says: *'Once Freddie went through the night for eight hours I knew he could manage it, so if he woke I ignored it. Now I only go in if he's hysterical.'*

Sue was breastfeeding Isabel, twelve months: *'She carried on waking for a feed once a night until very recently. Then one night she didn't wake up, it happened twice, then four nights on the run and that was it.'*

Can I encourage her to stop breastfeeding at night? – Many breastfed babies do wake in the night for longer:

Nadia, mother of Ben, now nineteen months, says: *'From one month to eleven months we went through hell. Ben woke four times a night. He went to bed at midnight, I fed and settled him and he then fell asleep on the breast or I fell asleep with him on the bed with me. It went on through the night and you feel you are doing something totally wrong but you can't help it.'*

If your baby has a quick suck and then falls asleep, she probably just wants comfort. Many babies eventually lose interest at night without any prompting – but if yours doesn't, and you are ready to give up, you can encourage the break. Let your baby linger over her bedtime feed (without falling asleep on the breast). Then, if you wish, give a top-up just before you go to bed. Take your time so your baby drains your breasts to get the really filling milk at the end of the feed.

During the night, your partner should go to your baby. Try offering one breast only or cutting down the time you offer each breast by about a minute on either side. If she starts to fall asleep, give her back to your partner to put back in her cot. If she cries, ask your partner to go in to her. If this gentle approach doesn't work for your tenacious baby, a solo weekend away may do the trick.

Will bottles help her to sleep through? – Bottle-fed babies may sleep through earlier than breastfed ones because formula takes longer to digest. Some (not all) mothers also find breastfeeding tiring. You have to weigh that against the evidence that breastfeeding boosts your baby's brain power (especially low birthweight babies), cements your bond with each other and protects her against ear infections, infections involving her breathing and diarrhoea. It's your choice!

Will solids help her to sleep through? – A baby between four and six months old who has been sleeping through the night but starts to wake hungry is probably ready for solids. Occasionally big three-month-old babies are also hungry – talk to your Health Visitor about it. If she isn't four months old yet, she will do better on a milk-only diet. But if she's in a growth spurt you can improve your breast milk supply by resting and letting her feed whenever she wants. Once she's four months or more you can give her a breast milk/formula-and-baby-rice mix or fruit/vegetable purée for tea to see if it helps.

Can I encourage her to stop bottle-feeding at night? – Once your baby is on three meals a day (and still drinking a pint of formula), you can cut down the night feed. Reduce the milk by an ounce a night until you get to an amount she always finishes. Next night put in less milk and top up with water. Dilute more until she's drinking water. Some babies do protest and this method does sound a bit unfair, but it's kinder than stopping abruptly.

Is a routine really so important? – Sleep habits have a lot to do with lifestyle. If you want to take your baby late-night shopping one night, out with friends the next and then stay in and watch videos the next – why not? Your baby may very well fit in.

But if she then can't settle to sleep she may be sending you a message that it's easier to have a predictable bedtime. That doesn't mean you have to sacrifice your social life entirely. At under six months it's quite easy to make compromises.

- Keep her up in the evening if that helps to guarantee you an unbroken night. *But try to make sure she gets to bed within an hour of the same time each evening.*
- Take her out and about with you. *But take a sleep kit too. It should include you or her bottle; her cuddly; if you like, a musical toy; night nappy; something familiar to sleep in. With this she can have a 'bedtime routine' wherever she happens to be.*
- Take her out to friends in the evenings. *But teach her first to fall asleep on her own or you'll spend most of your evening getting her off to sleep in her strange surroundings.*

What about sleeps during the rest of the day?

Try to keep her daytime naps reasonably regular and however tempting it is to get the morning chores done in peace, to get her up at a regular time. Some babies surface early, have a quick drink and then sleep until nine or nine-thirty. This may actually be a final burst of deep night sleep. If so, treat the early morning waking as you would any other night waking – with minimum fuss. Or bring your baby into your bed and cherish the chance to be close as you all drift awake.

If your baby sleeps too long and deep in the morning, try to wake her gently ten minutes earlier each day and if she's grizzly have a gentle game, take her outside or just stand with her by an open window until she feels better. Let her sleep as long as she wants at her next nap.

Key points

- Your baby can cope without a feed at night by six months.
- Breastfeeding's best for babies. But breastfed babies sleep more lightly.
- Routines help babies to sleep well at night.
- The most important part of the routine is bedtime.
- If your baby's four to six months old and she starts waking again at night, she may well be ready for solids.
- Keep to a regular getting-up time as well.

3
Settling problems

Wouldn't it be lovely if you could put your baby in her cot or let your child lie down in bed, say 'Night night', turn out the light and go? Yet many young children have settling problems and psychologists have found that as they get older these get more common. At nine months, one baby in five finds it hard to get off to sleep. Nearly half of all two-year-olds do.

If you think about your own baby or child, you may find one of the two scenarios that follow familiar:

1. 'I don't think she can go to sleep on her own'

In fact, she can. She does it repeatedly in the night (unless of couse she spends the whole night in bed with you). But the evening is more of an occasion and she's used to you being there. You may enjoy settling her down, patting and rocking her, singing her a lullaby and enjoying very tender gentle moments together. You may not mind dropping off yourself on the floor by her cot and waking up in the cold darkness! Or you may want her to settle but feel you can't be sure that she will be all right without you. There may be very good reasons for this:

- Your baby may have had a difficult start in life, as a premature baby or having been ill.

- You may have lost a baby before and so be especially anxious now.
- You may be an older mother whose baby feels especially precious.
- You may have felt abandoned by your own mother as a child – although these memories may be scarcely conscious.

If any of these ring true, do talk it over with your Health Visitor or doctor. It can be helpful to compare notes with other mothers with babies of a similar age.

2 She demands that I'm there while she goes to sleep'

Countless other parents have spent long evenings lying next to their babies and children, reading them the same story until they know it by heart, stroking, patting and rocking, scarcely daring to move as they watch the lids falter shut, and then creeping out holding their breath. Some never succeed in leaving; they spend the entire night with their child – just to avoid whimpers or screams of protest if they dare to try to leave.

It need not be like this. Your child has just got used to you being with her partly perhaps because she has a naturally obstinate or fussy temperament. But with planning, determination and support, you can give her the confidence to go to sleep on her own.

What to do

Remember: incredible as it seems, your baby or child will soon be going to sleep *happily* without you. The earlier you start (after the age of six months) the better, and it's certainly easier if your baby is still in a cot. If you're going back to work, do it *before* you return or when she's got used to her carer. Choose a time when there's nothing special on your calendar that might disturb her routine. Take a businesslike approach. Sit down with your partner, a pencil and paper and see what's going wrong. You might find it helpful to keep a sleep diary (see page 34) for a week – it helps to get it all in proportion. If you do, every morning write down the answers to the questions in bold type. If you're really keen, you can answer the other questions as well:

What happens now?

- **What time do you start to get your baby/child ready for bed?**
- **How do you wind down for the last half-hour?**
- Is there something she insists on doing every night? What is it?
- **What does your baby/child have to help her to settle to sleep?** Does she have a dummy? A bottle? A comforter?
- **Where does your baby/child fall asleep?** In your arms or do you nurse her? Is she normally downstairs with the rest of the family?
- **Does your baby/child fall asleep alone? With you close by, standing by her cot? In bed with you?**

Sleep Diary Please complete as soon as possible after each event

	Sunday	Monday	Tuesday	Wednesday	Thursday	Friday	Saturday
Date							
Time child got up in the morning							
Time, lengths and place of naps during day							
Time child taken to bed in the evening							
Time child eventually settled in evening and how you did it							
Time and lengths of waking in the evening and what you did							
Time and lengths of waking in the night and what you did							
As far as sleep was concerned, how did you find the last evening and night?							

- **How long does it take before she falls asleep?**
- How long has your baby/child been difficult to settle?
- What do you think started it?

Decide what you want to happen:

For example:

- Do you want her to lie quietly in her cot/bed until she falls asleep?
- Do you want her to go to bed with whoever puts her to sleep?
- Do you want to be able to go out in the evenings and leave her with a babysitter?

Write down what you'd like your baby/child to do

Now write your targets on a separate piece of paper and put it somewhere obvious, like on your fridge or by your calendar.

Try this approach

You want your child to know that her cot or bed is a safe, happy place to be alone. Once you get to the stage in her bedtime/settling routine where she's getting drowsy and you would normally try to get her off to sleep, you put her instead in her cot with her comforter and perhaps another cuddly toy and stay close by. Sit on a chair by her cot and tell her quietly and firmly to go to sleep. She may fall asleep or she may protest. If she gets up and rattles her cot bars or tries to climb out, wait till she flops and then firmly and confidently lay her down again. If she screams, wait for a break and then tell her in a positive tone of voice that she will soon fall asleep. Repeat 'Time to sleep' quietly and calmly. Avoid looking into her eyes and if you like pretend to fall asleep yourself.

This is hard on you, because you'll want to pick her up when she cries. Pat her, straighten her bedding, give her her comforter, but don't pick her up. It may take your baby half an hour or a few minutes to fall asleep but *once you've started don't give up*. Remember: if you have to start again, it'll be harder next time.

Once your baby has accepted this change, you repeat everything exactly the same next time, but with your chair a little further from her cot. Keep repeating the positive message that she will soon fall asleep. Every few nights move further away.

Occasionally you need to continue this until you are outside your baby's room. Once you are outside, reassure her with positive words, saying, 'Time to sleep.' You may need to keep on reassuring an older child until you are back in your own bed.

A step-by-step programme like this can take anything from a week to a month to achieve. If you take it very slowly, keep checking that you are still on target, and you may well need the support of a sympathetic Health Visitor or doctor. But stick at it. Don't give up. It does work!

If you decide that your baby can learn confidence more quickly than this, try sleep training instead, described on page 49.

But . . .

She really won't go to sleep – Is she tired? Was her last sleep too late in the day? Are you giving her a chance? She may well grizzle before dropping off and if she's older, she may scream and try to get out. Reassure her if she starts to get worked up. If she's still small, pat her in the cot or rock her gently. If she's getting really frantic, pick her up and hold her to you before laying her back. But do no more than is necessary for her to feel reassured. Then let her go to sleep.

She spins it out – This is standard older baby and child behaviour. She will not settle until you go back one more time, then you sing another song or read another story . . . Decide your absolute limits in advance – such as two stories and one good-night kiss. She will protest, but your firmness and consistency set boundaries that help her to feel secure. She will get used to it more quickly than you imagine.

Her father comes home in the middle, gets her overexcited and upsets the whole routine – One mother in this situation sent her partner off to the pub and wouldn't let him in until eight o'clock. That may be a bit drastic, but the message is plain. Fathers are adults too and should know that routinely disrupting bedtimes isn't fair. Either they get home earlier or bedtime waits for their arrival.

She'll only go to bed for me, not for her father – Some children accept small differences in routine better than others and the reason is probably that her father is doing things slightly differently. Some fathers are more lenient. Talk it over together when your child's not there so she won't pick up any tensions, and agree to follow the same routine.

- If you are still breastfeeding and giving a last comfort suck at night, give this outside the bedroom first. Breastfeeding isn't a good reason why your partner shouldn't put her to bed.

She drops off for ten minutes in the late afternoon and is set up for the evening – You may just need to keep her going until you're ready with her tea/bath/bed. These tricks work for some babies:

- Whooshing games – up in the air, airplanes, swinging from two adults' hands.
- Adults being silly – singing silly songs, balancing a pan on your head – anything will do, the more outrageous the better.
- Giving a slice of crunchy apple or a small stick of washed celery/carrot to eat. You can't fall asleep while munching.

Does she need a night-light in her room? – It doesn't matter. She'll get used to whatever you choose. Some parents close the bedroom door, some leave it open with the landing light on, others plug in a glowlight or use a lighted baby monitor. The important thing is that your child's room looks the same when she wakes in the night as when she went to sleep.

Separation anxiety

Any time between eight and ten months your baby may well become unspeakably clingy. If this wasn't so irritating (you can't even go to the toilet without howls) it would be flattering. But it's a normal stage of development (she may do it to your childminder or nanny if you're back at work) and will disappear if you go along with it during the daytime, either taking your baby with you or letting her follow you so she can see where you are and reassure herself that you are close by. In the evening it'll make settling more difficult for a few weeks and in the night your baby may want you. Reassure her by talking, or go in and stroke or pat her *without picking her up*. Remind her that it's time for sleep.

Comforters

Your child may well need a comforter – something to suck, cuddle or stroke. Not all children need them; many settle happily without one. However, other children go to extremes. A three-year-old child who took part in a study by psychologists in New Zealand took to bed with her three bears, a giraffe, a koala bear, an elephant, a rag doll, a red lambskin powder-puff and a mohair stole.

Psychologists call comforters transitional or attachment objects because they help to bridge the gap between being with a parent and being alone and between being awake and asleep.

But is one comfort object better than another? Should you encourage your child to suck her finger or a dummy? Comfort objects include clothes labels, rags, hankies, breast pads, cloth books, silky blanket edges, nappies and soft toys. Here are the most common objects chosen, with a few pluses, minuses and tips for each.

Thumbs and fingers

Plus

- 'She found her thumb at around two months and from then on it was plain sailing.'

- Your baby can find her own comforter without any help in the middle of the night.
- You can't lose it.
- You can wash it regularly without fierce protest.

Minus
- You can't throw them away.
- Intense suckers can make their thumbs and fingers sore.

Giving up – If your child is still thumb-sucking intensely when her permanent teeth come through at six or seven, she risks malocclusion – a gap in the bite of her top and bottom teeth. By this age you can set up a graded reward system for giving up: you go with your child to buy a really big prize, which you then put away in a cupboard. You also buy smaller prizes, which you give for the first day or two she succeeds in not sucking her thumb; then comes a prize for going a whole week without thumb-sucking and finally at the end of a month without thumb-sucking, she gets the big prize. She may still lapse if she is ill or under particular strain. But with a little extra encouragement (and even another prize) she'll maintain her success.

Dummies

'Louis came out sucking his thumb and stayed a sucky baby so he had a dummy. It was a nightmare because he would lose it and I had to spend half the night crawling around under his cot looking for it with a torch!'

Plus

- Wonderful for 'sucky' babies who otherwise stay latched to the breast.
- You have more control over its use than a thumb.

Minus

- More research is needed on dummy use, especially reported adverse effects on breastfeeding.
- Having to put it back in again umpteen times a night.
- Dirt.
- Dummy dependence – use it selectively for settling and soothing.
- Possible problems with speech – some speech therapists believe that dummies cause problems with articulation because they push the tongue out of place, making it hard to make sounds like *t* and *d*. Don't let a child talk with a dummy in her mouth!
- It looks awful!
- Possible difficulties with tooth alignment, but only if your child is still dummy sucking at six when the permanent teeth come through.

Giving up – Once the intense need to suck for comfort and food starts to wane around six months you can try to wean your baby off her dummy. Only let her have it at bedtime and take it out of her mouth once she's asleep. Alternatively, gradually cut down the times the dummy is produced, so your baby learns to soothe herself without it. Some children simply pop in a thumb or fingers when their dummy is removed.

Cuddlies [or comfort blankets]

Plus

- They can – usually – be taken away and washed.
- Children who have them are shown to be at least as sociable and well balanced as those who don't.

Minus

- They can fall out of bed and need replacing in the middle of the night.
- They can become unspeakably grubby before they are relinquished for a wash.
- They get lost.

Giving up – Why make her give up? There's no evidence that taking a cuddly away completely does any good. By all means keep it for home use only or just for home and car. But she's likely to grow out of it naturally or, by school age, be teased out of it by her friends.

> *'She's had her hankie since she was seven or eight months. We were going on an extremely long car journey and I gave her a hankie and it stuck. It's enough to sort her out if she wakes and grizzles in the night.'*

Do her daytime naps stop her from falling asleep in the evening?

Babies and toddlers need daytime naps, often until at least the age of two. You may be happy for your baby to drop off in the pushchair or car seat but most families find it easier to know when their baby is going to sleep so that they can plan their day. Babies who are unsettled sleepers find a predictable pattern of daytime naps especially helpful. If her last nap is too late (after 3.30ish) she won't fall asleep at bedtime, but no nap at all will leave her hyper and hard to settle.

The baby who doesn't seem to need a nap

Some babies are wakeful and don't seem to need a daytime nap. For your own sanity in the first year put your baby down for a short rest morning and afternoon. She may not sleep, but she'll rest and you'll get a much-needed break. Older babies sometimes won't sleep unless you lie down with them. Don't make a habit of it, but it might be a chance for you to get some rest as well.

Towards the one-nap-a-day toddler

There is a tricky time when your toddler needs more than one nap but less than two. If one nap has become longer, while the other is shorter and you can wake her quite easily from it, move things around a bit so that her one nap falls in the middle of the day but doesn't last too long into the afternoon. For a time it may coincide with lunch, but hunger will usually keep your toddler awake until she has eaten. As she'll fall asleep very tired, you may then need to wake her in the afternoon so that she has long enough up and playing before tea-time and bed for the night.

The 5pm nap

This is a risk zone for an older baby cutting down from two naps to one and again once a toddler's dropped her daytime nap but can't get through until bedtime. So what do you do? To cut down from two naps a day to one, try delaying her lunch-time nap start time by fifteen minutes a day or simply switching lunch-time so you feed her before her sleep rather than afterwards. Don't take her out in the car after 4pm and if you can, arrange your life so she has a quiet time from 3pm or 4pm onwards and doesn't reach tea-time overtired. If you see her dropping off, choose a quietly stimulating activity like going for a walk (not in the pushchair) or playing in the garden. She's likely to be grumpy while she gets over the feeling of tiredness, which may last twenty or thirty minutes.

Tracey, mother of Emma, then two and a half, says:

> *'I picked her up from nursery at quarter to six and desperately tried to keep her awake in the car all the way home with bribes and sweets and chocolate. If she slept in the car she was awake till ten o'clock. She was one of those*

children that ten minutes sleep could keep going for another three hours. That phase lasted for six months. Keeping her awake was Mummy being funny, Mummy singing out of tune, Mummy singing all the wrong words to songs that she knew.'

Key points

- Babies can settle themselves to sleep without you there from six months.
- It's easy to let babyhood habits continue so you go on settling your baby.
- You can start to train your baby to settle herself, starting today.
- It's kinder to everyone if you first train her in the daytime.
- You make sure she's content in her cot, then you leave her confidently.
- Comforters and cuddlies help your baby when you can't be there.

4

Waking in the night: the first year and beyond

Many parents – millions, probably – have found that they can train their baby to sleep through the night from the age of six months using simple behavioural methods. Instead of waking and being demanding, angry or just plain frightened, their children settle down again to sleep. When psychologists or specially trained Health Visitors use these methods, success rates are between 75 and 90 per cent. As no one knows your child better than you, there's no reason why you shouldn't have a 100 per cent hit rate. The sooner you take it on after six months the better.

The method is so simple:

- You let your baby settle herself to sleep.
- At the same time you make sure that she is all right *and*
- Let her know that you are close.

> Lucy, mother of Nicholas, twenty-six months, says: *'From six months I just left Nicholas to cry longer each time. By then I knew the type of crying that meant he was tired. I'd go in and check that he was OK and then leave him. The crying went on for five minutes perhaps. Doesn't it sound cruel? But it isn't and it works.'*

Think about what you do now when your child/baby wakes

Discuss it with your partner. If he's getting up for work next day he may be even keener to get on top of it than you. You may be able to answer the questions immediately, or it may be easier if you keep a sleep diary (see page 34). These are suggested questions, but the diary doesn't have to be complicated. Just keep a note of the questions below and your answers for a week. Just keeping the diary may help you cut the problem down to size.

- **How many nights a week does your child wake up?**
- **How often does your child wake?**
- **When in the night?**
- How do you know she's awake?
- **Who usually goes to her?**
- **What do you do and how long (in minutes) does it take?**
  Talk to her or pat her but leave her in her cot.
  Cuddle or pick her up.
  Give her a drink. How many bottles a night does he have?
  Give her a breastfeed.
  Lie down with her.
  Bring her into your bed.
  Sleep in another bed with her.
  Sleep in her bed.
  Anything else?
- **What time does she wake in the morning?**

Decide what you both want to happen:

For example:

- Do you want her to sleep from 7 pm until 7 am?
- Are you happy to have her in your bed from, say, 6 pm onwards?
- Are you happy for her to play in her cot if she wakes?

Write down what you'd like to happen. Write your targets on a piece of paper and put it somewhere obvious where you'll both look at it.

Start when:

- Your child already has a settling routine (see page 23)
- You are sure your child is:
  fed and able to get through the night without a feed
  warm
  comfortable
  dry (not potty-trained, though!)
  not having any great changes in her life
  secure in her relationship with you
  healthy – no snuffles, earache, teething or other disturbances.
- You are reasonably well rested; you have agreed with your partner what you are going to do; you don't have to get up early for the next two or three mornings (just in case you get very little sleep).

Wait until you can confidently tick off all these points. It's also easier if your child has a comfort habit.

Let's get on with it:
Sleep training – or controlled crying

Andrea, mother of Tom, four, and Louis, two and a half, says: *'I did it when Louis was ten months old and the crying didn't get to me so much. You've got to feel you're in control. If you are not, you get past dealing with it in a rational way. If they have boundaries they are more secure.'*

What to do

- When your baby wakes grizzling, wait for her to settle. There's a fine line between catching her before she goes over the top and leaving it too long, but by now you should know from experience.
- If it's clear that she's getting worked up, go in. This reassures your baby that you are still there and you reassure yourself that despite the crying she is all right. Don't pick your baby up, but straighten her bedclothes and touch her briefly. It's usually better to avoid eye contact. Once she has seen you and knows she is safe, you can go out. Say something simple and comforting but firm like 'Night night, time to sleep now.'
- Give her time to settle. Between two and five minutes is what most parents allow.
- Still crying? Pay another matter-of-fact visit.
- Still crying? Double the minutes before you go back in. Time it carefully. Then go in again in the same manner.
- Still crying? Bad luck! At this point it's important *not* to change your mind and scoop her out of her cot. If you do, she gets a muddled message. She might even think that the longer she cries, the more likely she'll get a reaction from you. Instead,

time the wait until your next visit to three times the original interval. Then visit her again in the same way.

- Still crying? No signs of tired whimpering or grizzling between the outbursts of anger? You're really unlucky. But do stick it out. Lengthen the interval before going in again. If fifteen minutes is as long as you think it's fair to leave a crying baby, keep returning at fifteen-minute intervals (no less) until she falls asleep. She will, but if she has a tough temperament or she's a child rather than a baby it may take an hour or two.
- If she wakes again later in the night, go to her again in the same way. This is hard on you – you will be tired. But she is too, so she won't take so long to settle.
- In the morning go in at normal waking time. If she cried for a long time before getting off to sleep, you may need to wake her, but otherwise you'll be surprised how happy and refreshed she is.
- Next night, treat her night-waking in the same way. Be careful to time the intervals before you go in to her so you don't unconsciously shorten them.

'We had two nights of hell and the third night he was sleeping like a god.'

Problems?

You may find the crying more upsetting than you expected – A few babies cry more for the first two or three nights than you expected. This can be extremely distressing, even if you know that it will lessen. You have two choices: either stop and try again in two weeks or a month or keep going for a set time – say, three nights, knowing that by then your baby will be over the worst. However, you must be sure that your baby is not ill, so always keep checking. *Don't* just give up for good or you'll lose hope that you can ever change your child's behaviour – and you can! If you fear that she will cry as distressingly the next time, try the gradual withdrawal method (see page 52). However, many parents find it too slow and prefer the 'Let's get on with it' approach.

> *'Sarah can scream for England and when she does her dad tends to cave in. But I look hard and don't attend to her unless I can see tears in her eyes.'*

Your child may cry herself sick – This is upsetting. Once you are sure your child is not unwell and is merely making a frantic bid for more attention, be calm and unruffled. Go to your child, change her clothes and bedclothes with minimum fuss, offer her a drink of water, then say 'Night night' and leave. If your child makes a habit of screaming herself sick, keep clean nightclothes ready and use a drawsheet on her cot. In the daytime, try to enjoy time together with your child and be especially careful to spend time with her at bedtime. If you need support to deal with this, contact your Health Visitor, doctor or local sleep clinic.

Your child may get up – Set up a safety gate at her bedroom door and reward her with small prizes for staying in bed. If she does come to you, don't pick her up (she'll think it's a cuddle and cling tight!) but take her firmly but gently by the hand and return her to bed.

She may wake up and get into your bed while you are asleep – When you wake, take her back to her bed, kindly but paying her as little attention as possible. If this becomes a habit, you may need a more secure method to persuade her to stay in her room.

She may cry for another reason – Once you know her cries well you'll recognize a cry of illness or pain. If your child is ill or feverish *of course* you must pick her up, cuddle her and see to her needs (see 'Common disturbances', page 55).

> Miranda, mother of Oliver, two, says: *'The controlled crying took longer than most people say, three or four weeks. At the time it seems like the cruellest thing in the world to leave your baby to cry. And there's the fear that it will damage him and he'll hate me. As soon as I left the room the crying started but we stuck at it. We were told that it would work and it did. Our breakthrough came the night when he screamed and screamed and then just fell asleep. Next morning he woke happy and didn't seem to remember the crying. Now he jumps into his own bed with great enthusiasm.'*

The tentative approach: gradual withdrawal

This is for parents who cannot face the distress of the abrupt changes that 'sleep training' can bring. It may be better for children over eighteen months or two years who have never settled themselves alone, for babies who cry themselves sick or are obviously badly upset by controlled crying. It is also more suitable for a child with asthma.

Gradual withdrawal is an adapted version of gradual withdrawal for settling (see page 35). It involves making small changes, gradually drawing back from your child while she learns confidence that she can fall asleep alone when she wakes in the night. It can take a long time, even months in an older child, and it is easy to lose patience. In this case, ask your Health Visitor for advice and support.

> A Health Visitor says: *'Make small changes, not sweeping ones, and remember that it can get worse before it gets better. Everything depends on how determined you are.'*

What to do

You reassure your child by letting her see you so that she knows she is safe but she then settles herself back to sleep alone. When your child wakes and cries, you put her back into her cot or bed and then go back to the place where you finally said goodnight at bedtime and say something firm and reassuring like 'Go to sleep, Daddy is here.' Then wait. If your child cries or screams, say 'Go to sleep' in a firm, positive voice. You then sit it out. Next time, you move one step further from her cot/bed.

Problems?

You're out of bed all night – You won't be. Half an hour is usually the most but even that may be too long in the middle of the night. If your child is very persistent, you may have to get up in shifts. You certainly need your partner's full support.

Your determination weakens – This approach can take longer to work than 'sleep training' and is especially wearing in the middle of the night. *Don't give up*, even if it means you fall asleep on the chair listening to the screams.

Your child won't allow you beyond a certain point – For example, your child may only allow you to sit on a chair just inside her bedroom door. Go one step closer for two or three nights so she knows that you are there and that she is safe. Make sure that the other times during the day when she separates from you are as happy as possible.

Night settling doesn't always work. Why not?

- *Are you really confident to leave your baby?* It may feel especially difficult to let your baby cry if she's been ill or was born premature. Possibly you are a lone parent or there may be personal reasons why she feels particularly vulnerable to you.
- *Do you feel that your partner supported you as much as you wanted?* Making a change calls for commitment from both parents. If one of you isn't ready, the messages will be inconsistent. Try again when you both agree.
- *Perhaps you have a difficult child. Some children are fractious, hard to soothe and resistant to change and take more effort from you to get to sleep.* The trouble is that the harder you try, the more they expect. So you can start out with a difficult baby and, in your desperate attempts to have at least some sleep, end up with a toddler who expects cuddles, patting, rocking and bottles to get to sleep and stay that way. Put another way, you end up with a difficult *and* manipulative baby. If your child fits this description, look again at the 'sleep training' suggestion (see page 49).

Common disturbances

Once your baby has got over the nightwaking, the last thing you'll want to do is disrupt it. But it happens all the time. Childhood has many inbuilt disturbances and when your child wakes and cries you have to strike a balance between letting her settle and losing sleep yourself. Sometimes the problem's clear – her bedding has slipped off, or she's thirsty and a drink of water is all she needs. Sometimes your child reacts to stresses at home, like a row, a parent going away on business, a grandparent or loved pet dying. But it isn't always obvious what's caused the disturbance. If your baby is behaving differently from normal, you should pay her attention, give her a cuddle and see to her needs.

Tracey, mother of Emma, four and a half, and Ben, seven months, says: 'Emma had phases when she'd be awake for a couple of hours in the middle of the night, perfectly happy if she was held but not happy if left in her cot. You'd think she'd be tired and go to sleep with no stimulation, but no. Ben's now started too. I panic when he starts. He's in the cot next to my bed. I try to ignore him but he rattles the cot and crashes about and starts to cry and if it's obvious that he's wide awake, one of us brings him downstairs to try to be quiet with him, just so the other can sleep.'

Teething

Your baby may start to be extra restless at night around six or seven months, when the first front teeth (the incisors) are coming through. However, you're more likely to be woken by the arrival of the first molars (soon after her first birthday) or the second molars (between twenty and twenty-four months). You'll see soon enough if teeth are causing the trouble; often your child's cheek is red on the affected side. Teething gels numb the gums for about twenty minutes, possibly long enough for your baby to fall asleep again. Rub a little on to the gums with your finger or a clean pad of cotton wool. Or try homeopathic teething granules. If your baby is clearly in discomfort, give her the full dose of paracetamol liquid. If she still seems restless or unwell in the morning, consult your doctor.

> Hazel, mother of Shannon, seven months, says: *'Shannon's had a wheezy chest and a runny nose since he was four months old but he coped with that until he started teething. He was really upset, but Calpol stopped the pain and helped him to settle down.'*

Colds

Surveys conducted for Karvol sleep clinics found that colds are by far the most common cause of sleep disturbance, especially when children start playgroup or nursery school. Keep the air in your baby's room reasonably moist (open a window or place a bowl of water near a radiator); gently clear secretions from the nose with a nasal aspirator (a small plastic pipette with a rubber bulb, like a medicine dropper) before sleep; tilt the head end of the bed slightly upwards by putting books under the feet or the mattress. Once your child is around three you can teach her to blow her nose, one nostril at a time. Before bed, give your child a warm bath or drink, as gentle steam helps to unblock stuffy noses. If this doesn't keep your child unblocked through the night, your doctor can prescribe paediatric nose drops containing a simple salt solution.

> *'If she had a cold sometimes I'd give her a bottle of warm water to drink for comfort and I got the impression that it helped to clear her nose as well.'*

Ear infections

Ear infections are a common cause of restless sleep. A baby with an ear infection will be miserable and fretful (with a cry you learn to recognize) and although she may drop off to sleep, eventually she'll wake again. If this happens in the middle of the night, give the full dose of liquid paracetamol. Warmth eases the pain, so lay a warmed cloth on the sheet or pillow or simply bring your child into your bed and let her rest her head, affected side down, against your chest. This also helps by raising her head; earache is worse when you are lying flat. In the morning consult your doctor, who will decide whether your child needs antibiotics.

Shelley, mother of Charlie, now two and a half, says: *'Charlie slept brilliantly until he was six months old. Then he started to get ear infections. They've continued ever since. You never knew whether he had an ear infection or not, but he could get two or three a month. Charlie has just had grommets put in and there's already a marked improvement in his sleeping. My Health Visitor said we should wait until he had grommets before working on his sleeping patterns.'*

Eczema

A baby who is rubbing or scratching may have eczema, made worse by the warm bedclothes and, possibly, the house dust mite. To help, keep your baby's skin well moisturized with bath oil and aqueous cream, perhaps also with calamine. Use cotton bedclothes and nightwear and, if need be, tape cotton mittens to your baby's hands. Don't overheat her room and keep it well ventilated. If the eczema doesn't get much better, or if you think it may be linked with your baby's food or milk, consult your doctor. He might prescribe a mild cream containing hydrocortisone to control the inflammation.

Nappy rash

A baby with a sore bottom obviously won't sleep soundly. Some babies have especially sensitive skin; others develop a rash when they have a cold or are teething.

To help prevent and treat a rash before it disrupts your

baby's sleep, use a good-quality night-time nappy. If this doesn't help, show your doctor. It might be a candidal rash (bright red, shiny, itchy) and need a mild antifungal cream perhaps containing hydrocortisone.

Snoring

One child in ten snores and for most – four out of five – it doesn't matter so long as no one else wakes. But in a tiny number of children snoring is part of a condition named obstructive sleep apnoea syndrome in which the child occasionally stops breathing very briefly. She starts again naturally on her own, but the repeated breaks disrupt her sleep. So if your child snores and seems tired during the day, talk to your doctor. Decongestants might help, or possibly surgery.

The next baby

The birth of a brother or sister is disturbing for the older child. It's worse if:

- the older child is in his own room and the baby is with you
- the older child was wakeful at night before the baby was born
- the older child has recently moved to a bed
- the older child has recently started childcare or nursery
- there have been other big changes in his life, such as you stopping work and being at home for him all day
- you had to spend more than a night or two in hospital for the birth

Keep your child's daily routine as familiar as possible; spend time with him during the day and devise 'big child' privileges. If you hand over bedtime and staying in bed responsibilities to your partner, check that he is being as firm as you would be. Don't fall into the trap of always quietening the baby in case she wakes your older child as you can end up with two wakeful children. It's surprising how little a baby's crying will normally disturb an older child.

Helen has two children, Anna, twenty-seven months, and Andreas, ten months: *'Anna was very good until Andreas was born but now she wakes every night and comes to our bed at 2.30 or 3 while we're asleep. After the birth she became terrified of going to bed so I started to lie with her telling her stories until she went to sleep and then I crept out. I'm still doing it! Anna strokes my hand to be sure I'm still there for her. I try to make sure she's asleep before I leave but she still wakes up. It started when Andreas was in with us. I hoped it would disappear but I think it's getting worse.'*

Holidays and moving house

After moving house or going on holiday, expect your child to need extra time to settle and to need more reassurance to go up to bed on her own. But so long as she is content and feels safe in her own bed, she'll overcome her fear of the new surroundings. The following is one mother's practical solution.

Lucy, mother of Nicholas, twenty-one months, says: *'We take Nicholas everywhere with us. With his sleeping bag that has his own familiar smell, his toy and his musical mobile he'll go to sleep anywhere. I try to take him away with us regularly because his memory is so short. It's to keep him flexible so he can fall asleep anywhere.'*

Key points

- If your baby wakes at night, you can train him to sleep through.
- Training often only takes two or three nights.
- If you don't want to hear your baby cry, you can use a gentler method of gradually withdrawing, but it takes longer.
- Once you've got your baby into good habits, it's easier to start them again after she's had an upset like a cold.

5
Sleep and older children

Once your child is two or three you will probably find that her sleep problems lessen. She sleeps longer at night as she drops her daytime naps and if she does wake in the night, she's better at looking after herself. Instead of being woken by a wailing 'Mu-u-mmy!', you can hear the sounds of slurping as she has a drink, then a brief conversation with her 'friends' in her cot before she falls asleep again.

Her bedtimes too will probably fit in with yours now. Some families are happy to spend their evenings together and let their children fall asleep downstairs before carrying them gently to their cot. If this fits in with your lifestyle, that's fine. Even the mornings, though often still earlier than you'd like, become manageable at this age. Many families enjoy waking together in the same bed, especially on leisurely weekend mornings.

If your child's sleeping isn't quite as straightforward as this, and you'd like things to change, you may find that they do naturally. As your child goes to toddler group, playgroup and then nursery her day will become more organized and often her nights will fall into line as well.

Even if they don't, you now have the advantage that you can talk to your child, tell her what you want, ask her for her views and agree what you want to happen. Even if she isn't at nursery yet, you can tire her out physically during the day so she sleeps better at night. And she'll be more amenable to rewards (or is it bribery and corruption?) to help her change her ways.

But the big change at this age is the move from a cot to a bed.

Out of her cot and on the run?

You'll move your child from a cot to a bed when she starts to get uncomfortable in a limited space or learns to climb out. If you want to be sure she doesn't fall out of a bed, choose one with built-in bars, like one half of bunk beds that separate, or use a bed guard. Many children sleep just as soundly in a bed – some even better, as they have more space to wriggle – and don't make use of their newfound freedom. But when they do, it's worth making clear what you want to happen.

- Childproof her bedroom, especially the windows. If she comes out of her room, put a stairgate at the top of the stairs.
- When she gets out of bed, take her back, saying firmly but not angrily that it's time to sleep. Don't settle her again as if it was bedtime or take her into bed with you or she'll learn that getting up is rewarding. You may have to take her back time and again for a few evenings before she accepts.
- Think of ways to encourage her to stay in her room, such as a tiny present at breakfast or under her pillow in the morning. If this doesn't work, try:
- standing outside her door and holding it shut until she agrees to stay in bed.

- if you think she is anxious, try sleeping on a mattress outside her door. She knows she is safe but she can't come out.

Your child will need a signal when she can get up in the morning and leave her room. You could hang a smiley face outside your bedroom door; put a clock radio in her room timed to come on quietly at waking-up time; put a timed light by her bed. You may feel driven to lock in an especially difficult child. However, you shouldn't do this as it can make her very anxious and there is a fire risk. Instead, contact your Health Visitor, doctor or local sleep clinic (see also page 108).

- *Tip:* Moving a younger child in with an older child? Keep your younger child in her cot until they are used to sharing.

Tracey, mother of Emma, now four, says: *'When Emma was two and a half we moved from a flat to a house so she got her own bedroom and a bed instead of a cot. She was fine for a while but by the autumn when it got cold and she couldn't pull the covers back over her, she'd come into our bed. She used to come in while we were sleeping so there was nothing we could do about it. In the end we stopped it with bribery. Emma had discovered sweets and the love of her life was lollipops and to get one she had to stay in her bed. It worked very fast and now she doesn't ask for them any more; it's become entirely natural to her that she stays in her bed.'*

Wakeful children

By the age of two to three, your child will often need around twelve hours' sleep a night. But many children need much less – just eight or nine hours – and just a few need less than their parents. Allow a wakeful child to have quiet toys in her cot although always double-check first for safety. By three or four, many wakeful children enjoy books and a few learn to read quietly while you sleep.

Some children are very active in their sleep and while it's one thing having a warm bundle next to you in bed, it's quite another having a wriggling, clinging, stretching and kicking child. Restless or light sleepers sleep better in their own beds in their own rooms, because adults disturb them and they disturb adults. Use a reward system (see page 70) to encourage your child to sleep in his bed or use the gradual withdrawal method (see page 52).

Tiring a child out is a good way to help her to sleep well. Try to go out every day, especially if you don't have a garden. Keep your child's diary full of regular physical and social activities (toddler groups, music and movement, gym class, swimming or just going to the playground), always allowing for a late afternoon wind-down so that for the last hour or two activities are gentle. Once your child is at playgroup or nursery, you don't need to make such an effort, but make sure the holidays are full of activity. Don't give your child tea or cola or any other caffeine-containing drink if you notice it keeps her awake.

Waking early

'Martha would wake at five or five-thirty. In the early morning, there's nothing on the telly, it's dark and it's cold. At first we used to take her into our bed but she then started to wake in the night to come in with us. We tried everything, early nights, late nights, bringing her in with us in the morning, giving her a bottle of milk – but nothing worked. She would come into my bed and Paul would move into the other bed. In the end you don't care. You just want to sleep and you'll tackle the behaviour later. I remember watching a video of Barney in the early hours and thinking, I'm going to shoot myself.'

Many children wake ready for games while their parents are fast asleep. First, check for obvious things:

- *Could it be the early morning light?* Make sure that the curtains in her bedroom are thick enough.
- *Could it be a noise?* A child who is just waking is sensitive to noises. It could be central heating noises, traffic or refuse collections, even birdsong.
- *Is she kicking off her bedding and getting cold?* Dress her in a sleepsuit or use a continental sleeping bag.
- *Is the early morning call really a middle of the night disturbance?* This can happen to children who go to bed at the same time as their parents and never learn to soothe themselves. You will know if you have this type of child because after a brief play she will settle down again for a long sleep, effectively finishing off her own night. Treat this type of disturbance as you would any other night waking.
- *Has she slept enough?* Persuade her to amuse herself in her cot

or room until you are ready to get up. Leave a leakproof lidded cup by her bed, either with water or very well diluted juice. Once she is potty-trained, leave a pot. Leave books and safe, quiet toys. If she has slept enough but you aren't confident to let her play alone, keep a box of soft, quiet toys in a corner of your room. You can doze while she amuses herself.

You may be happy for your child to come into bed so long as it's not at four-thirty or some other ridiculous hour. Even before she can tell the time you can help her to know when she can come in and when she can't. Use an alarm clock or put a sidelight in her room on a timeswitch and once she's in the habit of responding to the timed signal, bring it forward by ten- or fifteen-minute intervals. Make her welcome when she comes into your bed as this is her reward for being good.

From the age of around four she can even watch a video or children's TV (starting at 6am) from her own bed. Load the video the night before so that all she has to do is turn it on.

Put your baby and child in together. They may play and 'chat' while you doze.

Late bedtimes

You may be very happy for your child to go to bed at the same time as you if you are a working parent and want to see your child during the week, if you are from a background where a long afternoon siesta is the norm, or if you don't want to be woken with the dawn.

But late bedtimes have drawbacks. What if you and your partner want an evening to yourselves? What if you want to go out? Or what if she won't go to bed until after your bedtime? Children of three and four still usually need eleven or twelve hours' sleep, so they must either be in bed by early evening or have a daytime nap. Once your child starts nursery and later school she will be tired, especially if she's one of the four-year-olds coping with a full day in a reception class. You may well need to cut down her social activities during the week to allow for a quiet resting time when she gets home. Your child should now be in bed by six or seven, but if she is showing early warning signs of sleepiness (thumb-sucking, twiddling hair, getting fractious), start your bedtime wind-down straight after tea.

Don't forget the elements of a good bedtime: tea, play, ten-minute warning, tidy toys away, upstairs (no chasing), bath (and no more coming downstairs now), pyjamas, drink, story or lullaby, bed, 'Night night' kiss.

'She's wide awake at bedtime'

This usually means your child is over-excited. Family homes are busy places in the evenings with older children coming home, friends coming to play and mums busy cooking tea. It's easy for your child to get excited just when she should be calming down. Just occasionally there's a more complicated explanation. After a holiday or an illness your child's biological clock gets out of sync so she goes to sleep late and wakes late. You'll know if this has happened because your child will fuss and resist when you put her to bed and then be overtired and bad-tempered in the morning. But if you put her down to sleep later, she'll go off without a struggle. The cure is to bring forward *both* getting-up times and bedtimes by ten or fifteen minutes a day until she's back to her normal habits.

'She doesn't like me leaving her'

If your child's an anxious sort, she may not like you going away. Let her choose a toy to take to bed with her, go through your normal 'Night night' routine and then leave. Tell her what you're going to do (make it boring, like tidying the living room or sorting the washing) and in two or three minutes put your head round the door to see if she's all right and so she sees you. Just say something like 'Night night, Mummy loves you' and leave again. Come back after three minutes and continue until she is asleep. Over the days, lengthen the gaps between visits. Within a week or two she'll probably be able to fall asleep without any reassuring visits.

- *Tip:* Don't send her to her bedroom if she's been naughty during the day. If she needs punishment, let her do 'time out' in the hallway or other neutral territory. You don't want her to link her bedroom in her mind with being punished.

Changing bedtimes

- Decide when you want your child to go to bed and wake up. For two or three days note down when she actually does.
- Plan to change her bedtime by thirty minutes on the first day and then fifteen minutes every second day.
- When you start the change, follow her usual bedtime

routine and get her to sleep at her normal time. Wake her at a regular time in the morning. The parents of one child who was very grumpy in the mornings used to let the cat into his room to wake him.

- Come evening, watch for signs of tiredness. Once they show, start the bedtime routine.
- If you aren't in a hurry, just change bedtime by fifteen minutes every week. She'll barely notice.

Prizes, rewards and star charts

Over the age of two or three you can use positive rewards to encourage your child to sleep well. Then she will link doing what you want with what she wants. So choose a reward she really wants – not all children care about stars or smiley faces on a chart. When you're starting something new (like staying in her bed all night) you'll need to reward her every time she does it; but once she's in the habit she'll just need occasional reinforcement. Agree with her (include her in the planning if you want it to work!) a series of small clear targets such as going to bed without crying or getting up only when the light goes on. Reward positive behaviour (staying in bed) rather than negative behaviour (not disturbing Mummy and Daddy). Extend the achievement (staying in bed all night) and give a larger reward (a special trip with Daddy; a new video) for this. Praise her and make her feel good about her reward; eventually the feeling of pride will take over from the need for collectables.

After a week she probably won't need rewards any more. However, if she starts getting up again, reward a good night.

- *Tip:* Keep your prizes small or buy remaindered toys to avoid bankruptcy.
- *Tip:* If your child doesn't attain the planned target one night, don't let her bargain with you or reset your standards to allow her to get the reward. Instead, plan together for the next night.
- *Tip:* Don't remove privileges.

Medication

Doctors generally agree that apart from special cases (such as learning-disabled children) sedatives don't help sleepless children. Occasionally, though, sedating a child can help parents in crisis, so do discuss it with your doctor. He may still suggest sleep management first, but he might prescribe a sedative for a few nights to break the habit and give you a rest.

You can buy the following medicines that may help from a chemist:

Paracetamol elixir (such as Calpol) – *not* a sedative but by far the most popular choice. The pain-killing action and sweetness may indirectly promote sleep.

Teething preparations (such as Dentinox) – again, *not* a sedative but a painkiller.

Antihistamines (such as Phenergan) – not for children under two; they can make your child restless and the effect wears off quickly.

Paracetamol plus antihistamine (such as Medised) – popular, but not suitable for babies under one.

Bedwetting

Between three and five years old most children become dry at night. In the early days children have a lot of accidents and some wake when they wet the bed. Others wake afterwards when they are cold and know that a wet bed is one reason you *will* come to them at night. But most bedwetters stay asleep.

So how can you help?

- Don't be impatient to get your child out of night nappies. Some children are ready after a few months of daytime dryness at the age of three, but many are not. Even by the age of five, one child in six is still bedwetting. As she can't control when she's dry at night, there's nothing to be gained by getting her out of nappies too soon.
- Encourage her to drink plenty during the day, but only if she's thirsty at night-time. Depriving childen of daytime drinks doesn't keep them dry at night – but overloading their bladders at night is asking for trouble.
- Drinks containing caffeine (colas, coffee, tea) or fizzy drinks can make bedwetting worse by stimulating the kidneys to make extra urine, so if your child drinks them, watch out for effects.
- Once she is out of nappies, teach her to use her potty alone and leave it on a non-slip surface by her bed. Protect her bedding – a drawsheet or bath-towel over the middle of the bed is useful – and leave out dry pyjama bottoms and pants.

Keep the heating on low in her room at night so the cold doesn't put her off getting out of bed. Check that she isn't frightened of the dark or of creatures under her bed – all good reasons to stay snug under her duvet!

Some young children become dry at night and then relapse. There can be lots of reasons for this – the stress of a new baby, the challenge of starting school, a sad event in their lives, or nothing that you can identify. If you know what the stress is, do what you can to eradicate it. Then use praise and rewards (see page 70) to encourage your child to stay dry.

Juliet, mother of Katy, three, says: *'Katy knows I'll come to her if she says she needs a wee. It's the only time I take her out of the bedroom at night, to sit her on the loo and then put on a fresh nappy. But I keep it pretty brisk because I don't want it to go on.'*

Angela, mother of Nathan, five and a half, says: *'Nathan had been reliably dry for a good eighteen months when he started bedwetting. His pants were soaking in the morning. At first I thought it was a one-off, but after two weeks he was no better. Then I realized why. His father had gone away on a business trip to America for ten days. Nathan was never especially close to his father, but the wetting started the first night he was away. Unfortunately, it took six months before Nathan had another dry night.'*

Key points

- If you're firm and determined, your child won't disturb you any more when she's in a bed than when she was in a cot.
- It's best not to have wakeful children in your bed, but there's lots they can amuse themselves with if you have to.
- With a timed device you can teach early wakers when it's OK to disturb you in the morning.
- Once you've got a bedtime routine in place, you can bring it forward gradually so your child is fresh in the morning for childcare or nursery.
- Prizes and rewards are good for keeping your child's sleeping habits as you want them.
- Medicines don't cure bad habits but they can give you a break.
- Let bedwetters become dry in their own time.
- Don't let fear of bedwetting be the one reason you will go to your child at night.

6
Special situations

Your family situation can be make-or-break if you have a child with a sleep problem. Here are three common family situations that parents of sleepless children find themselves in.

Lone parents

There's nothing about being a lone parent that makes it more likely your child will have sleep problems. But the whole weight of sorting them out falls on you.

> A Health Visitor says: *'I feel very sorry for single parents. It is even more important for them to get a good night's sleep so that they can cope with the next day. They also need time for themselves in the evenings. Yet their accommodation is often far from ideal and they have worries about their neighbours. Imagine trying to get a young baby into a sleep routine in a bedsit!'*

'When he wakes in the night, there's only me. I'll do anything for a quiet life'

Short-term, being constantly overtired because of your child's night-waking makes you irritable and negative. Long-term, it drives you into feelings of depression.

Solutions include:

- Taking a 'crying till he crashes' line from the start.
- Bedsharing.
- Asking a grandparent or other relation who's fond of your baby to take over for one or two nights a week.
- Getting a friend in to share the nights.
- Sharing babies with a close friend. You do night duty for both babies while your friend gets some sleep. Then you swap.

'I can never get out in the evening. He's always awake'

Evening wakefulness is common practice in young children, whether they have one or two parents. But your evenings matter more if you are on your own, especially when you're with your child all day. You need time off – and babysitters don't relish wakeful children.

Solutions include:

- Starting a firm bedtime routine now (see page 21).
- Taking your baby out with you. Great at first, especially if you're breastfeeding. But eventually she gets too big, her equipment gets too cumbersome, she needs a quiet place to sleep in and you need time away.
- Swapping babyminding sessions with friends. If there are five

or six of you, you can run a rota or do individual swaps. You can get out in the day too.

'The walls are paper thin. I can hear the neighbours' TV so I can't let him cry himself to sleep'

Where you live may not be ideal. Tiny rooms, shared bedrooms, bedsits and thin walls make everybody's life more difficult but there'll be something you can do.

Solutions include:

- Double-carpeting the floor and even running carpet up the walls to deaden noise.
- Putting your baby in the hallway/bathroom/kitchen.
- Letting her cry in the daytime when she won't annoy the neighbours so much.
- Letting her learn to settle at your parents' or a friend's house.

'I've got a new partner'

If your child takes against your new partner or finds herself displaced from your bed, there will be difficulties.

Solutions include:

- Handle it like having another baby. Teach your child to sleep in her own bed (see page 63) before your partner arrives, leaving at least a month between your child moving out of your bed and your new partner arriving.
- Agreeing with your new partner to share the getting up at night. It's worth a try!
- Spending extra time during the day with your child so that she feels reassured. It's a difficult time for her.

Parents' experiences

Angie, single mother of Tony, three and a half, says: *'I sleep with Tony because it's the only way I can be sure to get some sleep, but if it gets too bad, I call my mother, who lives in the next road. Tony goes to bed on his own but usually gets into my bed at three. I don't sleep very well because I have to hold him in. He puts his arms round my neck, gives me a big cuddle and a kiss and though I'd rather he didn't, I haven't got the strength to take him back. And if he's hard to handle during the day, it's a way of keeping a good relationship with him. In the morning before the television goes on it's so quiet and lovely, we lie there and have a little chat together.'*

Lisa, single mother of Ruby, three, says: *'I don't have a sex life to ruin. Anyway, if Ruby has decided she's coming in with me I couldn't take her back to her room if I handcuffed her. At weekends I really love us being in bed together. She has her bottle and we both lie in bed and watch the cartoons on TV.'*

Sleep and the working parent

Parents out at work all day have bonuses – you can tap into the experience of your childminder, nursery or nanny to learn the no-messing way to do things. Because you have to get up for work your child will have a routine for each day. And you're likely to be businesslike about sleep. But it isn't all good news.

A Health Visitor says: *'Working mothers can feel guilty about leaving their children and this gets in the way of establishing a calm regular bedtime routine. It cuts both ways – on the one hand they don't want the short quality time they spend with their children to be a time of distress so they give in to them more quickly; on the other hand they are more determined to see the sleep problems through because they know they can't hold down a job and deal with a sleepless child. A lot of parents come to see me when their baby is eight or nine months, saying, "I've got to get him to sleep because I'm going back to work."'*

'I want to go on feeding her at night but it's so exhausting'

Some mothers only return to work when they've phased out the night feed and the waking that goes with it. But you may want to continue with that night feed. In a busy week it may be your only time together in skin-to-skin contact, allowing a physical closeness that can be 'banked' for the next day apart. It also helps you to make enough milk if you are expressing and storing during the day.

Solutions include:

- Continuing breastfeeding but not keeping your baby in bed with you. You'll probably sleep better.
- Savouring the evening feed and giving a morning feed to empty your breasts – but skipping the night feed.
- Giving a feed just before you go to bed.

'I'll be too tired to work properly'

Compared with staying at home and looking after small children, parents go to work to put their feet up! But this is a serious issue.

> 'As a parent, you always work at a certain level of tiredness but you are able to rise above it at work. However, when it catches up with me, I under-perform. I forget to do things, but I was lucky, I went back when my daughter was one. That's not half as bad as if you go back after three months.'

Or try this for a solution.

> Juliet, an art dealer, says: *'I went back to work at ten weeks while I was still breastfeeding and was completely exhausted. I got just one thing done in the morning and one in the afternoon and then I was so tired I went to the toilet, locked the door and lay down on the carpeted floor and slept for half an hour. It got much better after I gave up breastfeeding.'*

'We're with her for so little of the day that we want bedtime to be nice. But every night we have tears and tantrums'

It's easy to be out of sync with your child at bedtime. She's ready for bed – overtired, possibly – while you're tired but ready for quality time. Or a ten-minute snooze on the way home from nursery or the childminder has set her up for the evening while you have housework, shopping and cooking to catch up with. Perhaps you've brought work home with you.

The one thing your evening doesn't hold is any time for yourself.

Solutions include:

- Doing everything you can think of to stop her falling asleep on the way home 'The Five o'clock nap' (see page 44). If nothing works, remember it's a temporary phase, or consider home-based childcare.
- Being entirely at your children's disposal once you're home. The shopping and housework can wait.
- Being extra firm about bedtime and not allowing her to spin out the 'Night night' time. Sixty minutes is enough for the entire process. Any child under two or three who is looked after by someone else during the day knows how to settle herself to sleep. Day nurseries are often especially good at teaching effective sleeping habits. Copy them at home – your child is capable of calming herself.
- Reaching a compromise with your partner if you don't agree bedtime policies. Either you both follow the same policy or you take a block of evenings each. Sharing out evenings during the week muddles your child.
- Making sure her daytime separations are good. If your child is unhappy at separating during the day, her unhappiness may spread to cover bedtime. If you have any doubts about the quality of your childcare, address them.

'It's difficult to have a routine when weekdays are so different from weekends'.

A key to decent sleep patterns is a regular day–night routine. If your child's routine changes dramatically at weekends, her sleep is likely to be regularly disturbed.

Solutions include:

- Following the routine she has in daycare. You'll sacrifice a weekend lie-in but your reward might be peaceful evenings and nights.
- If you don't want to run your home like a mini-institution, your child will eventually come to accept the inconsistencies. You can always resort to under-the-belt bribery like promises of early morning videos if she goes to bed and stays there.

Parents' experiences

Michele is a solicitor with two daughters, Siobhan, two years, and Roisin, twelve weeks. Michele went back to work full-time five months after Siobhan was born and is now on maternity leave again. Siobhan has always been an especially wakeful child.

> *'Bedtimes could last a long time. I'd return from work at six-thirty and Siobhan would come back from her nannyshare shortly afterwards. She was quite tired so we'd read stories and have a bath, aiming to finish by eight, then we'd do things like close the curtains, put on her pyjamas, play her music sleep tape and have a drink of milk. Getting her to sleep might then take five minutes or an hour and a half, depending on her mood. She'd want the same story again and again. Then we'd have lullaby songs and more stories and she would lie in bed while I sat with her. But if I tried to slip out I'd hear, "Where are you going, Mummy?" I was trapped!*

'It was quicker if my husband did it. He thought that was because she wanted me and said she should be allowed compensations for the fact that we didn't see her during the day. Siobhan would then wake twice during the night.

'You can also guarantee that if you have a bad night the next day at work will be hectic. If I have to be up at six for work, Siobhan will wake at four. She can sense it. Does it affect my work? If I'm tired, instead of doing things automatically I have to think about them. But it's the response of your colleagues, especially women without children! They are not one bit sympathetic.'

Twins and more

If you are pregnant with twins or more you may well be worried how you're going to cope. But the news is reassuring. When the Twins and Multiple Births Association surveyed 600 members it found that almost one in three of their children under three years were waking at night. That rate is close to the numbers of one- to three-year-olds identified by the Royal College of Psychiatrists as having sleep problems. And the numbers of families with persistent wakers were also very similar. It seems that twins plus don't sleep any worse or better than other babies. The problem is what it always is with twins and more – you have double the trouble (and twice the joy!).

'How can I possibly have a routine when I've got one baby in hospital and one at home?'

You can't. In the early days, don't worry about routines and bedtimes. Once both your babies are home, you can wait for a routine to emerge and build on it. It *will* happen and there *will* be an end to the broken nights, although if your babies were premature, you must allow for that. If you have someone to help you, try to ensure consistency by each doing the same jobs every night so the babies learn who to expect. If you're managing alone, you can split up the bedtime routine so that you do part of it together (say, feed and cuddle) and part of it separately, putting the sleepier baby down before the more wakeful one. You may find your babies are more relaxed if they have separate baths. During the day, put both babies down to sleep at the same time.

'How do I feed two babies at night?'

All babies need a night feed until four to six months. Yours may need one for even longer and may wake (or need waking) at first for a feed. Perhaps wake them for a feed before you go to bed. Have the babies in your room (possibly sharing a crib or one in a cot and one in a Moses basket, whichever suits them best) and feed them at the same time if you can or one after the other if you can't. If you feed one first, make sure you know which twin you have fed; it's easy to forget in the night-time blur!

'We don't have the space for them to have their own room each'

Twins often get on well sharing a room. Far from disturbing each other, they offer one another comfort and company. With older twins be careful what activities you allow in bed or they won't get the 'It's time to unwind' message. Reading is usually OK but not playing.

Sometimes a single wakeful twin sleeps better in a room with an older brother or sister who sleeps well. To avoid bickering if your twins don't share a room, read the bedtime story on neutral territory (the bathroom, your bedroom) or swapping nightly between bedrooms.

Deborah has twin daughters Sophie and Laura, twenty months. She says: *'They were born at forty-one weeks, weighing 5lb 14oz and 6lb 5½oz and were breast- and bottle-fed from day one. Laura was the quieter twin and was always OK so long as she had a dummy. But Sophie has a different personality and would spit a dummy out. From day one she cried a lot and the crying brought out the monster in me. I remember shouting and other things you don't dwell on.*

'My husband did night duty and the night feeds as much as he could but I was only coping by my fingertips. I didn't want sleep problems and by six months I knew Sophie didn't need a drink so I thought I would get on top of it early and we followed the controlled crying programme. Sometimes our resolve wasn't textbook and the first night Sophie screamed for one and a half hours – but she didn't wake Laura. The second night was better because she knew I

meant business. It felt like hell letting her cry – I thought she would hate me but next morning she woke bright and happy. Ten days later she was sleeping through and I felt wonderful!'

'Won't one of them wake the other when he cries?'

Leave them together until you are sure that this happens; it is surprising how often it doesn't. From day one, settle them back in their cot without picking up, rocking or cuddling so that they learn to fall asleep on their own. A dummy can prove a lifesaver.

'But one of them *does* wake the other'

React fast. If this gets out of hand, you face two equally impossible scenarios – two children screaming in the middle of the night *or* one child who knows you'll move heaven and earth rather than let her wake the other twin. Move the better sleeper out temporarily while you run an intensive sleep training programme (see page 49) on the other. It may only last a night or two; at the most a week. Alternatively, put them in separate rooms – but not in yours. If there's nowhere else, use the kitchen, hall or bathroom. One couple decamped downstairs while their twin boys took the two upstairs bedrooms. The arrangement lasted for a year and a half until the boys were over two.

Juliet, mother of twins Katie and James, now three, says: *'Katie woke at nights ready to party and as there were a couple of famous occasions when her screaming woke James, which made it ten times worse, not waking him became a priority. So Katie could be up partying from two until five. Twice I took her to the bathroom and put her on a towel on the floor and lay down beside her and fell asleep.'*

'We end up with at least one in bed with us'

In some families only one baby may want to share your bed but in many it's both. Two babies and two adults in one bed doesn't usually work for long; instead they separate out to an adult plus a baby in separate beds – not very good for your relationship! If you only need to take your baby in with you occasionally, it may be the right answer. But you need to sleep and there's always the possibility that your baby views bedsharing as a reward for crying and cries harder. It's better to comfort him in his cot or bed if you can. But see Bedsharing (page 11).

Key points

- Having difficult circumstances at home may make you more brisk and businesslike about sleep problems.
- However you may need extra support.
- The difficulties every parent faces, like waking at night and not having free evenings, can get on top of you so don't be afraid to ask for help.
- Find other mothers in your position.

7

Dreams, nightmares and sleep terrors

Most young children behave oddly sometimes while asleep and some children go through worrying phases, doing things like mumbling or waking night after night from bad dreams. You may worry that your child is upset about something. Sometimes a stressful event or an illness can start the odd behaviour at night, but it's rarely a sign of anything deep seated. These strange forms of sleep behaviour are usually thought to be caused by a mismatch between sleep states, with part of your child's mind behaving as if asleep while another part behaves as if awake. However, do talk to your doctor or sleep clinic if you are concerned.

He's frightened

And he's not alone! It's why we put night-lights in our children's bedrooms, give them furry toys to cuddle and check on them after we've left them to go to sleep. Fear in the night probably affects all children. But while most children learn to cope, in quite a few, perhaps one or two out of every ten children, the fear becomes a real issue. Pre-school children are most often scared of large animals, monsters and dogs, of losing their parents and being alone. Your child may be frightened to get out of bed because something is hiding underneath it or in the wardrobe. Some of these fears embody anxieties and worries from the day that take on physical form when your child is tired.

Go upstairs with your child and think together what would make the darkness more manageable, such as a story tape or simple things like checking that your child is all right half an hour after you say 'Night night'. You may be surprised how sensible your child's suggestions are.

When you leave, reassure your child that he is safe and you are nearby. Tell him what you are going to do next. If you are going out and planning to leave him with a babysitter, let him meet the babysitter during the day when he isn't tired so at bedtime he can picture someone familiar. Leave his room as he'll find it when he wakes in the night. If he has a night glowlight to fall asleep with, leave it on all night. Most children like the door left open to allow light through from the landing, but some can conjure monsters out of the spooky shadows!

Studies show that you can do lots of things to help acclimatize children to what scares them – you can reward them for facing their fears, simply tell them to face up to them, or teach them to flout fear by saying something like, 'I'm OK, I'm really brave!' In one study, a group of three- to six-year-olds were helped to handle their night fears by learning to relax and image a pleasant scene and then repeat to themselves, 'I am brave. I can take care of myself when I am alone. I can take care of myself when I am in the dark.' Every night the child coped with his fear, he got a token. Ten tokens and he got a special outing.

Funny waking

I don't know how else to describe these episodes, but they are pretty common, especially in babies and toddlers. Your baby may start moving and thrashing about and then get more worked up and cry. He seems to be awake but if you try to calm him, he doesn't seem aware that you are there. Intervening may make him even more agitated. It's best just to stay close by for the five to fifteen minutes your baby will take to calm down. Technically, these funny wakings are called confusional arousals.

Sleeptalking

Sleeptalking is almost standard in young children, sometimes starting even before your child can talk! It occurs while your child is in light dream sleep as well as when he is in much deeper sleep stages and if you can hear what he is saying, you may recognize snatches of recent experience. It is absolutely nothing to worry about and your child will fall silent as abruptly as he started talking.

> Naomi, mother of Tom, four, says: *'Tom has always talked in his sleep. Even before he had speech he would make long noises while he was asleep. Then about three months after*

his brother was born, when he was twenty months old, his speech became more upset and frightened until he was screaming in his sleep. Sometimes he'd be wide awake, other times he wouldn't be. I'd pat him and calm him and that was enough to send him back to sleep and eventually he grew out of it. When he was bitten in the back at nursery it sparked a particularly bad episode.'

Sleepwalking

Sleepwalking isn't what it looks like, a Lady Macbeth-style playing out of dreams. A sleepwalking child isn't dreaming at all, but is in the deepest non-dreaming stage of sleep. Your child is completely unaware of you during the episode and remembers nothing or has only a vague memory of it the next day. Sleepwalks usually last for five to fifteen minutes (it can be as long as thirty minutes) and no more than one session a night is the general rule.

Sleepwalking is surprisingly common – especially where there are other sleepwalkers in the family. One study in Sweden found that over 35 per cent of children had sleepwalked at least once and most research agrees that as many as one-third of all children have frightened their parents rigid by getting out of bed and moving automaton-like around the house while obviously fast asleep. Sleepwalking isn't linked with serious emotional problems in your child's life although stress and anxiety can make it worse. Children grow out of sleepwalking by their teens or before.

If you find your child sleepwalking, don't try to wake her. She would be very hard to wake as she is so deeply asleep. However, at one level, you will find your child responsive. Quite a few children get dressed and put on their shoes before their tramp round the house but are quite co-operative about taking them off again. If you take your child gently by the hand and lead her back to bed she's unlikely to resist. However, if you talk to your child she won't answer clearly enough to be understood. Stay with her until she falls asleep, which is usually quickly.

You're right to worry whether she'll sleepwalk while you are asleep, so fit a stairgate at the top of the stairs and remove anything she could trip over from landings and corridors, as well as locking all upstairs windows. One family stopped their child from wandering the house by putting a large armchair in his doorway. It was enough to wake him as he tried to squeeze past it. If the sleepwalking is becoming very frequent, you can try stopping it by noting what time in the night your child usually gets up and then waking her gently fifteen minutes beforehand, every night for a week. It often puts a complete stop to it.

Nightmares

Fiona, mother of Natalie, now four and a half, says: *'Natalie comes into our bed and says she's had a bad dream. She started talking about her dreams some months ago when she was three and a half or four, and she had occasional nightmares. The night before last it was triggered by a picture of a zebra with large plate-like eyes in a book she didn't like – she didn't even want to look at the picture.'*

It's extremely likely that every child has bad dreams but only some have nightmares (bad dreams that wake them). But they're pretty common – one recent study in Reading found that one-third of four-year-olds had had a nightmare in the previous six months and one child in seven had frequent nightmares. The dreams actually occur during light REM (dreaming) sleep and when your child wakes she is responsive, if upset and frightened. In the morning she may well remember some of the nightmare of the night before. Nightmares can arise when your child has a high temperature, or if she's had a recent upset that's made her anxious. Sometimes nightmares relate to something that happened the day before or to a frightening video or picture in a book.

Reassure and comfort your child in her own bed until she falls asleep again. This way she will associate her bed with safety and your presence. If she wants to tell you about her bad dream, listen but don't pressure her to talk.

Recurrent nightmares

If your child is having frequent nightmares, ask yourself what the cause might be. Reassure her that she is perfectly safe and that it is only a dream. Some children find that a 'magical' cure dispels the nightmare, but it's actually better for your child to learn that she can have some control over the experience herself. Let her talk about it, act it out or draw it during the day. Think about other ways the bad dream could end; or what she could say to frighten whatever is scaring her away. Make sure your child's wind-down to bed is calm (no scary videos or even TV news) and relaxing (no bursts of violent exercise). If the nightmares are always about the same thing, it might be worth mentioning them to your doctor as your child may have an anxiety she can't cope with.

> Lucy says: *'Nicholas started to have nightmares when he was about eighteen months old. His cry from his room is different, it's a panic cry and instead of quietening down he gets more frantic. When I go in, he's usually awake and standing up in his cot. I pick him up, cuddle him, talk to him to distract him from what's on his mind and perhaps give him a drink. Not too long, then I put him back down and stroke his head until he goes to sleep. I might leave the light on a little brighter when I leave. He seems to have a nightmare every three weeks or so and it usually seems to be linked with something that happened the previous day.'*

Sleep terrors

Picture it – you are woken in the late evening by a scream from the bedroom, anything between an hour and three hours after bedtime. You rush in to find your child, typically four or older, sitting bolt upright in bed, terrified, her eyes wide open. She may be sweating and shaking or out of bed and moving around. But she doesn't recognize you or respond to you. This is a sleep terror.

Sleep terrors affect more children than you'd imagine – anything from one child in 100 to one in twenty-five. They are more common in boys and although the cause is not clear, there may be a temporary abnormality in the deepest slow wave sleep. There's disagreement among researchers as to whether stress or anxiety brings on night terrors, but whatever the cause, they almost always disappear by adolescence and often well before. They are caused by the same sort of arousal that causes sleepwalking.

Faced with a child having a sleep terror it may seem unreal to suggest that the best approach is to stay calm – but it is! Don't try to wake her or you can make her even more distressed. Your attempts to soothe her may well go unheeded, but just stay with her and try things like a low light in the bedroom or a gentle, familiar tape. By all means try to settle her back into bed. Within twenty minutes she'll be sound asleep again and you can go back to bed without worrying because it is highly unusual for more than one terror to follow in the same night. Next morning you may still be shaking with the memory but your child will remember nothing.

Contact your doctor for help and support – not because the terrors are serious (in the end your child will simply grow out of them) but because they are so disturbing to watch. If your child has a series of terrors, 'waking treatment', devised by Dr Bryan Lask, consultant psychiatrist at Great Ormond Street Hospital for Sick Children, may be recommended. For five nights you note what time your child has a terror and whether you can see her move and twitch beforehand. If you can see a pattern developing, you wake her ten to fifteen minutes before you expect the terror to start and keep her awake for five minutes. Repeat this for five to seven consecutive nights and you can often stop the terrors altogether. Some parents have noticed that you can also cure a child of terrors by making a change to their routine, such as changing bedtime, bedrooms, or going on holiday.

Just an hour after dropping off to sleep, four and a half year old Ryan used to wake every night screaming, sweating and shaking. He muttered and pointed to invisible objects, then cowered behind his hands as his mother Marion tried to comfort him. All she could do was wait for the terror to go away. The wait could be as long as five minutes and seemed like an eternity. Ryan's terrors started out of the blue, Marion's doctor suggested the waking treatment, which was an instant success. When Ryan's terrors started again, Marion tried waking him and keeping him awake for at least five minutes. She made sure he was with it, gave him a drink and told him a story. Then she settled him back to sleep. Ryan hasn't had a terror for three months.

Head-banging and other rhythmic behaviours

Head-banging, body-rocking, or rolling are the most common types of rhythmic behaviour that children indulge in as they get themselves off to sleep – and sometimes while they are asleep as well. They are all transitional states and no one would give them a second thought if they weren't so distressing to watch.

Rhythmic behaviour tends to start around your baby's first birthday, often as body-rocking, and most children have outgrown it by the age of three. It is three or four times as common in boys as in girls and research has shown that in young children it is *not* linked with any behavioural or emotional problems. However, it may increase at times of stress.

It is perplexing to know what children get out of their behaviour, but it is clearly pleasant or they wouldn't go on. Researchers have suggested that it is like the experiences of dancers rhythmically moving to music. Children who continue head-banging up to an age when they can describe it confirm that it is nice and they sometimes use it to help with pains like toothache and headache.

It is usually best to let children grow out of the behaviour naturally. If they do not, ask for professional help. Even severe head-bangers can be helped by behavioural treatment involving a mixture of recording what is happening, followed by something offputting (making it unpleasant, uncomfortable or difficult to head-bang) and something to reward them for stopping.

Key points

- Children – and adults – can behave very oddly when they are asleep but there is only very rarely a deep psychological reason.
- You can teach a child to take control of her fear of the dark.
- About a third of children sleepwalk, especially in sleepwalking families. They outgrow it, but it's a good idea to make your home safe.
- All children have bad dreams and most have nightmares. Ask a doctor's or Health Visitor's advice if your child has the same nightmare again and again.
- You can prevent sleep terrors by waking your child fifteen minutes before they are due.

- Body-rocking and head-banging are a bit like having a comforter – they help your child to get off to sleep. Your child will outgrow it but if it upsets you ask a doctor's or Health Visitor's advice.

8

Sleep and special needs children

Sleep problems can be especially grinding in children with long-lasting conditions and while other children grow out of them, in children with special needs they are both more severe and tend to persist. Children with Down's syndrome and cerebral palsy are affected as well as the groups of children considered here. According to the charity Sleep Scotland, sleep disorders are a major cause of stress in special-needs families, leaving them more prone to break down.

Any family with a special-needs child who suffers from a sleep disorder should be supported by their doctor or a specialist sleep clinic. This section can only give descriptions to show you are not alone and general guidance. If you have a child with special needs, live in Scotland and need further advice and support, contact Sleep Scotland (see 'Who can help', page 108). Families come to them with children with autism, Asperger's syndrome, cerebral palsy, ADHD, learning disabilities and Down's syndrome as well as less common conditions.

Jane Ansell of Sleep Scotland says: *Every parent knows that their sleep gets disrupted by young babies. The difference with special-needs children is that they don't grow out of it and that the techniques the books tell you to try don't work where your child's mind is operating on a different level . . . When three-year-old Jacqueline wakes up she insists on stripping all the beds – regardless of whether her little brother is still asleep or not. She switches on the video and fast-forwards to her favourite parts. She pulls chairs into lines, empties cupboards and winds the curtains round and round. The magic of our approach isn't teaching parents skills they probably know anyway, but the support and commitment of sleep counsellors far as long as it takes to improve the child's sleeping pattern.*

Children with learning difficulties

Glenys Sykes, Health Visitor, says: *'On the whole children with learning difficulties are older before they start sleeping properly and their parents accept their sleep-disturbing behaviour for longer, sometimes until it is intolerable. To take control, parents have to be extremely firm and have a clearly set routine.'*

Severely learning-disabled children may have a sleep–wake cycle that's quite irregular or doesn't match the twenty-four-hour clock. To make matters harder for their parents, the sleep problems tend to stick. But why? Dr David Bramble from the Child and Adolescent Psychiatry Unit at the University of Nottingham says that ninety-five per cent or more of children including severely learning-disabled children are physiologically capable of sleeping through the night at six months of age.

One cause is that learning-disabled children don't pick up the cues about daily patterns of living that other chidlren do, so their sleep–wake cycles don't become 'socialized'. They may not remember so well from one day to the next. To help, your doctor may well prescribe a sedative, which can be a lifesaver. Yet many parents find that the sedative doesn't work or the effect wears off rapidly or their child becomes excited instead of sedated.

An adapted version of sleep training (see page 49) works well instead. You'll know what sleep training involves. Try this:

- Deciding on a regular bedtime and sticking to it.
- Establishing a wind-down routine before bed.
- Getting your child into a sleepy mood just before bedtime.
- Quickly settling your child in her bedroom and particularly avoiding any argument or protest.
- Leaving the bedroom and turning out the light.
- Ignoring your child's protests unless there is evidence that she is ill or extremely upset.
- Telling your child to go back to bed or taking her back if she comes out.

Although you may worry that this absolutely-no-nonsense approach can verge on the brutal, recent research by Dr Bramble has shown that it's the approach parents of severely sleep-disturbed children are happiest with. Rapid settling, he says, hasn't been shown to have any important harmful effects.

Children with autism

Autistic children also have irregular patterns of sleeping and waking, particularly when they are younger. There is probably a direct link between the child's developmental level and his sleep disturbance, so more forward children sleep better. But older, more able children can be prone to anxieties, which makes falling asleep difficult. Problems get worse if your child's environment changes suddenly or when his childcare isn't consistent.

But the normal behavioural approaches, firmly applied, appear to work best. This story shows what you can achieve if you're prepared to be firm.

> Rollo is three and a half; he is autistic and has asthma. He also has two older brothers and his mother, Maura, is a lone parent. *'Until a month ago we thought we had it taped. Rollo didn't sleep but he just used to bang and rattle around in his cot. Then he discovered how to climb out. It was too dangerous to leave him so we put him in a cot bed and the first night was disastrous. He pulled everything out of his wardrobe and got out the nappies and shredded them. So now I have stripped his room, locked his wardrobe and screwed it to the wall and left him with nothing but his Teletubbies and duplo. Next he found that he could reach the windows by climbing on the radiator knobs, so we've stuck a cupboard in front. We lock his room at night and in the daytime he has a babygate at the door. The first night I locked him in he screamed for an hour and then woke again at two o'clock and the next night was hardly any better. I just waited until*

it was quiet and crept in and he'd pulled his mattress on to the floor and was asleep on it with no bedding. I don't move him as I don't want him to wake up. I just leave him. I know he's absolutely safe. There's nothing in his room he can damage or break and if he's noisy, I can hear him on the monitor.

Your child needs individual solutions. These examples come from the *Parent Survival Manual: a guide to crisis resolution in autism and related developmental disorders:*

- A young child who wouldn't sleep in bed but liked music and rocking. His mother put a rocking chair and music in his room. Gradually he learned to move into bed as he felt sleepy.
- A girl who was ultra-sensitive to noise. Her parents carpeted the floor and one wall and insulated the room as well as installing a machine that made water sounds.
- A five-year-old who wouldn't be covered by blankets. Her parents covered her dolls with blankets. A few nights later the girl covered her dolls and then herself.
- A four-year-old boy who wouldn't stay in his room. His father removed the door handle from the inside of his room. Other parents fix double handles, one out of the child's reach.

Children with ADHD

Some hyperactive children sleep especially well. But an overactive or hyperactive child who *also* has a sleeping problem can make your life very difficult. And if your child is short of sleep, his inattention and impulsiveness will certainly get worse.

Hyperactive children find calming down at the end of the

day very difficult. You need an extremely firm end-of-day routine and you must stick to it. Build in bedtime rituals (one story, a song, a last cuddle) because they may not occur to your child. Some hyperactive children feel really anxious when you go. (See 'Sleep terrors', page 94, for ways to help.) In the UK the stimulant drugs used to treat ADHD are not recommended for children under six but in older children they can cause sleeplessness. Yet a stimulant drug solved six-year-old Justin's sleep problems.

> Barbara Tuffill, a psychiatric nursing assistant, adopted her grandson Justin when he was eighteen months old. *'We never had a complete night's sleep. He'd wake six, seven or eight times a night and slept in a travel cot by my bed so I didn't have to get up. When he became mobile as a toddler it became really difficult. Getting him to bed was very hard. I'd lie on the side of the bed and pretend to snore; later on I introduced a relaxation tape. We did try leaving him to cry but that exacerbated the whole thing. He'd bang and shout and scream for an hour or so – you can't leave that going on. In the end what solved it was being put on Ritalin at the age of six – he slept and we all got a night's sleep.'*

Children with asthma

You can't just ignore a child with asthma who wakes and cries at night. And it is very likely that they will. When Dr Greg Stores, child psychiatrist at the Park Hospital, Oxford, recently measured sleep in children with asthma, he found it was very fragmented. The children woke briefly (for less than two minutes) between eight and seventeen times a night and on average four times for longer spells. The children were then, not surprisingly, sleepier in the daytime and found some learning tasks more difficult. Once the asthma was better controlled, the children woke much less often.

So keeping your child's asthma well controlled will not only help her and you sleep through the night, it will also improve your child's mood, thinking ability and behaviour. If your child has asthma and wakes repeatedly coughing at night, you should visit your doctor to have her medication reviewed.

You may get the asthma under control but find that your child still has sleep problems. Before you decide to follow a sleep-training programme, you should contact your doctor. He is most likely to advise gradually withdrawing attention at night rather than a sleep-training programme.

> Craig, 5, has had asthma since he was a few weeks old and his mother Sharron has not had a full night's sleep since he was born. *'Before he was diagnosed, at nine months, I just used to take him into bed with me and that's what I still do if he's bad. When he was alone in his cot the coughing and crying was worse. Then he was prescribed an inhaler, so when I heard him coughing, I'd get him up, give him the inhaler and stay with him until he calmed down. But he was still coughing and it seemed as if I was up all night. He was given steroids and his coughing at night is better now, but his body clock is set to wake twice a night out of habit, first at around twelve-thirty or one o'clock and then again around five. I take the inhaler up with me every night just in case and if he wakes, it's only*

> *for five or ten minutes. I tried to leave him to cry a couple of times but we were up most of the night instead of for five or ten minutes. I couldn't now because I'd feel so guilty if he had a bad asthma attack.'*

Gifted children

One consoling thought for parents is the possibility that their bright and alert if sleepless toddler might in fact be a high-IQ wonderchild. The research evidence linking low sleep needs with intelligence is equivocal, but according to clinical and educational psychologist Dr Ludwig Lowenstein, who claims to have seen at least 500 high-IQ children, there is a clear link.

> *'At least three-quarters of the parents of the children I have seen say their children sleep very little, sometimes as little as five or six hours and significantly less than their parents. They try to wear them out and keep them amused and stimulated, but it doesn't always work.'*

Professor John Williams, a retired psychomathematician with an interest in low sleep needs and high IQ, thinks the egg may need to be placed before the chicken: children who need little sleep simply get more stimulation because they are awake for longer.

Whatever the case, the blessing for parents of MENSA candidates is that their children are likely to learn to read early, often at the age of three. From then on, they can read away for hours while their parents are asleep.

Key points

- Children with special needs seem to have especially difficult sleep problems.
- That's probably because they don't learn what's expected of them as soon as other children.
- They do best with an extremely firm and clear approach.
- Their bedrooms may need to be made especially safe.
- There may also be physical reasons why they sleep less well.
- If the physical problems are corrected, their sleep gets better.
- But sometimes they need training to improve their sleep.

9

Who can help?

Your Health Visitor may well run a sleep clinic for parents of babies and children just like yours. Your doctor should be able to refer you to a specialist sleep clinic.

Serene is a support organization for parents of crying babies and babies with sleep problems. Contact Serene at BM Cry-sis, London WC1N 3XX or the Cry-sis Helpline, 020 7404 5011.

The **National Childbirth Trust (NCT)** offers information and support in pregnancy, childbirth and early parenthood, as well as antenatal classes and breastfeeding counselling, it has a network of postnatal support groups. If you need more information, telephone 0870 444 8707. Or write to the NCT at Alexandra House, Oldham Terrace, Acton, London W3 6NH.

Sleep Scotland currently offers advice and support to families of special-needs children with sleep problems living in Scotland. Contact Jane Ansell, Sleep Scotland, 8 Hope Park Square, Edinburgh EH8 9NW. Tel: 0131 651 1392. Email: sleepscotland@btinternet.com

BLISS 2nd Floor, 87–89 Albert Embankment, London SE1 7TP. Tel: 020 7820 9471.

TAMBA, the Twins and Multiple Births Association, runs a helpline, Tamba Twinline, a national confidential support and information service for parents of twins, triplets and more. It's open weekdays 7–11 pm and weekends 10 am – 11 pm and is staffed by parents of twins, triplets and higher multiples. Tel: 01732 868000.

The Multiple Births Foundation publishes a booklet 'How do you get twins (or more) to sleep?' Price £2.50 plus 50p postage and packing from the Multiple Births Foundation, Queen Charlotte's and Chelsea Hospital, Ducane Road, London W12 0HS. Tel: 020 8383 3519.

The National Autistic Society has a helpline, 0870 600 8585, open weekdays 10am–4.00pm. 393 City Road, London EC1V 1NG. Tel: 020 7833 2299.

For information on sleep in children with Down's syndrome, contact The Down's Syndrome Educational Trust, The Sarah Duffen Centre, Belmont Street, Southsea, Hampshire PO5 1NA Tel: 02392 824261 (available as Adviceline Thursday 2.30–5.30 pm). Email: enquiries@downsnet.org

Books

Many of the ideas described in this book have come from or been adapted by parents from books. If you'd like to read more, try:

Clinical Handbook of Sleep Disorders in Children, ed. Charles Schaefer (Jason Aronson, 1995)

The Good Sleep Guide for You and Your Baby by Angela Henderson (ABC Health Guides, 1997)

Three in a Bed: why you should sleep with your baby by Deborah Jackson (Bloomsbury [due for reissue 1998/9])

Why We Sleep: the Functions of Sleep in Humans and Other Mammals by James Horne (Oxford University Press, 1988)

Solve Your Child's Sleep Problems by Richard Ferber (Dorling Kindersley 1986

The Parent Survival Manual: a guide to crisis resolution in autism and related developmental disorders by E. Schopfler (Plenum Press, 1995)

Coping with Children's Sleep Problems – a Talking Life tape produced in association with the Royal College of Psychiatrists, 1997.

Articles from the following journals have been useful:
Acta Paediatrica; *Archives of Disease in Childhood*; *Archives of Pediatrics and Adolescent Medicine*; *Child: Care, Health and Development*; *Developmental Brain Dysfunction*; *Early Human Development*; *European Child and Adolescent Psychiatry*; *European Journal of Pediatrics*; *Journal of Advanced Nursing*; *Journal of American Academic Child and Adolescent Psychiatry*; *Journal of Child Psychology and Psychiatry*; *Journal of Developmental and Behavioural Pediatrics*; *Journal of Pediatric Health Care*; *Journal of Pediatric Psychology*; *Journal of Pineal Research*.

SUBSCRIBE TO PRACTICAL™ parenting magazine

& SAVE UP TO 25% TODAY

Practical Parenting magazine has the most comprehensive, trusted, up-to-date information and advice for every stage from pregnancy through to pre-school.

Enjoy all these subscriber benefits...

- **Great savings off the cover price**
- **FREE postage and packing**
- **Guaranteed delivery so you never miss an issue**

PLUS it's a great gift idea for family and friends!

ORDER HOTLINE NUMBER 01622 778778

(Lines open 7 days a week 9am-9pm)

Call the orderline now and quote 29M for your special offer.
(Order before August 31, 2001 and save up to 25%)

Or you can write to us at:
Practical Parenting Subscriptions
FREEPOST CY1061,
Haywards Heath, West Sussex RH16 3ZA, UK